THE OFFICIAL itv SPORT

EURO 2012 FACT FILE

Euro 2012 Stars • Euro 2012 Action • Euro 2012 Fun

Nick Callow

CARLTON

Contents

Left: Scenes of celebration as Spain are crowned European champions in 2008. Who will be lifting the Henri Delaunay Trophy in Kyiv in 2012?

Introduction

The whole of Europe has been desperate for this tournament to start ever since Andres Iniesta scored the winner in the 2010 FIFA World Cup, and there is one simple question on everyone's lips – who can stop Spain?

It will be absolutely fascinating to see if the best managerial brains in Europe have come up with a way to stop Xavi, Iker Casillas, Cesc Fabregas and friends.

The Spanish are, after all, bidding to become the first side in history to win the UEFA European Championship two years before and two years after the FIFA World Cup. They were crowned European Champions after beating Germany 1–0 in the final in Vienna four years ago, followed by victory, again 1–0, but on this occasion after extra time, against the Netherlands in Johannesburg in 2010.

And those two sides are the favourites to challenge Vicente del Bosque's men this time around – although you can never rule out the likes of France, Italy and, of course, England.

It promises to be a fascinating tournament, and this book will tell you all you need to know – and more.

For a start there is a guide to every one of the 16 teams, their captains, coaches and star players. So while you might know about Wayne Rooney or Wesley Sneijder, could you pick Alan Dzagoev or Anatoliy Tymoshchuk out of a line-up?

Don't forget, every European Championship turns some players from low-profile professionals into household names. Maybe it's the turn of Christian Eriksen or Wojciech Szczesny to show their skills to a wider audience? You can learn all about them here.

Above: Kyiv's Olympic Stadium will be filled to capacity on 1 July when the Euro 2012 final is played there.

But the real stars of the show should be the host countries. Poland and Ukraine are desperate to put on a tournament to remember, and with good reason. Both countries have four host cities each, and have shrugged off prophecies of doom that said they wouldn't be ready in time. One look at the newly built stadiums in Kyiv, which will host the Final, Warsaw and Poznan proves that the facilities will be first-class.

Then it's all up to the people everyone really wants to watch – the players.

The European Championship has created a number of stars in the past, from Marco van Basten to Rooney, and we are all expecting the football to hit the heights this summer.

And if you're not excited then just look at the Groups. There can scarcely have been a more fascinating pool in European Championship history than Group B, which features Holland, Germany, Portugal and Denmark. There is no room for error there!

England also face a tough task, having been drawn with France, Sweden, and co-hosts Ukraine. Can the Golden Generation at last become winners? The whole country will be hoping that the Three Lions can win their first international trophy since 1966 – while the Republic of Ireland are sure to be entertaining in their first European Championship appearance for 24 years.

But if that doesn't keep you entertained then there are a number of puzzles and quizzes in this book that will do, as well as a chart to track how each team is getting on.

It should be a summer to remember!

Happy reading.

Welcome to Poland and Ukraine

Poland and Ukraine will welcome the whole of Europe to UEFA Euro 2012 – and you would struggle to find prouder hosts. Their joint bid blew judges away when the Finals were awarded, beating bids from rivals such as Italy and Croatia-Hungary.

The countries have promised a warm welcome, spectacular stadiums and a football festival to remember in June.

Part of the appeal was to take the Finals to eastern Europe, behind the old Iron Curtain. Ukraine regained independence from the Soviet Union in 1991 but has a history dating back to medieval times.

Euro 2012 is a chance to put itself not just on the football map (clubs Shakhtar Donetsk and Dynamo Kyiv have already done that) but on the political map too – and to attract millions of tourists in future. Matches will be held in Kyiv, Lviv, Donetsk and Kharkiv.

Famous Ukrainians include classical composer Tchaikovsky, author Nikolai Gogol, boxing champion brothers Wladimir and Vitali Klitschko and the world's greatest-ever pole-vaulter Sergei Bubka.

And then there is Andriy Shevchenko! Sheva, once European Footballer of the Year, is determined to prove Ukraine deserves its place on the highest stage – having helped his team to reach the FIFA World Cup 2006 quarter-finals.

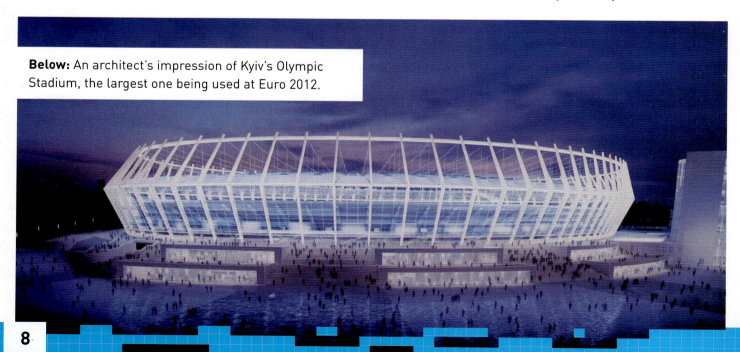

Below: An architect's impression of Kyiv's Olympic Stadium, the largest one being used at Euro 2012.

Local food favourites include borscht (a type of beetroot soup) and why not try a Chicken Kiev in the city in which it was given its name?

Poland has more than 1,000 years of history and is one of the most historic names in European football. It broke away from the Soviet Union in 1989 and its football history includes finishing third at the World Cup in 1974 and 1982. Legends include many who have played in England – such as Liverpool's Jerzy Dudek.

And other famous Poles in history include multi-gold-medal Olympic sprinter Irena Szewinska, Formula 1 driver Robert Kubica, composer Frederic Chopin, scientist Marie Curie and Pope John Paul II (Karol Wojtyla).

Fans travelling to Poland (games are staged in Warsaw, Gdansk, Wroclaw and Poznan) can look forward to amazing Gothic castles like the Teutonic Knights' Castle at Malbork and city centres that are a combination of medieval history and modern architecture.

The national diet features a meat-based stew, "bigos", and soups including meat or vegetable dumplings called "pierogi".

Leading clubs in Poland include Wisla Krakow, Legia Warszawa and Lech Poznan – whose fans first invented the crazy "backs facing the pitch" celebration. So, it looks like it will be party time in Ukraine and Poland for UEFA Euro 2012.

Meet the Mascots

Say hello to the smart new mascots for UEFA Euro 2012 – Slavek and Slavko! Their names were chosen after more than 20,000 fans voted to choose their favourite – and you'll be seeing a lot of them during the tournament.

It's easy to work out who is who: Slavek will be decked out in Poland's national colours of white and red, while Slavko will wear the national colours of Ukraine which are blue and yellow. The pair have even dyed their hair in national colours to show their support!

The mascots were designed by the film-makers Warner Bros and they will tour Poland and Ukraine to meet fans and cheer on their teams.

They should prove to be important members of the Euro 2012 squad, but don't get the twins mixed up! Slavek wears the number 20 shirt and carries a ball in his right arm, while Slavko wears number 12 and has the ball in his left arm.

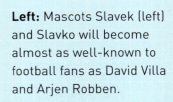

Left: Mascots Slavek (left) and Slavko will become almost as well-known to football fans as David Villa and Arjen Robben.

Euro 2012 Venues

The venues for the UEFA Euro 2012 matches have been split evenly between Poland and Ukraine with four stadiums hosting games in each country. The Final will be held at Ukraine's impressive Olympic Stadium in Kyiv – complete with a transparent roof.

Right: Kyiv's Olympic Stadium will be packed with 60,000 fans for the UEFA Euro 2012 final.

Poland

Municipal Stadium Gdansk
Club: KS Lechia Gdansk
UEFA Euro 2012 capacity: 40,000

Gdansk will play host to a quarter-final as well as group games and the stadium will be one of the iconic sights of UEFA Euro 2012. Its exterior is designed to resemble amber – which is mined all along the Baltic coast.

Games:
10 June: Group C, Spain v Italy
14 June: Group C, Spain v Rep of Ire
18 June: Group C, Croatia v Spain
22 June: Quarter-final 2

Municipal Stadium Poznan
Club: KKS Lech Poznan
UEFA Euro 2012 capacity: 40,000

The Municipal Stadium is famous for generating a ferocious atmosphere and is one of the biggest club grounds in Poland. Getting there should be no problem – it's very close to the city airport!

Games:
10 June: Group C, Rep of Ire v Croatia
14 June: Group C, Italy v Croatia
18 June: Group C, Italy v Rep of Ire

National Stadium Warsaw
Club: None
UEFA Euro 2012 capacity: 50,000

The new home of the Poland national side, this stadium was built on the site of the old Tenth Anniversary Stadium on the banks of the River Visztula and is designed to resemble a fluttering Polish flag. It will stage the opening game, a quarter-final and a semi-final.

Games:
8 June: Poland v Greece
12 June: Group A, Poland v Russia
16 June: Group A, Greece v Russia
21 June: Quarter-final 1
28 June: Semi-final 2

Municipal Stadium Wroclaw

Club: WKS Slask Wroclaw
UEFA Euro 2012 capacity: 40,000

Another clever design, the newly built Municipal Stadium looks like a Chinese lantern. Situated alongside the Sleza River, the surrounding complex includes a casino, fitness centre and club museum. A new tram line makes access to the stadium easy for fans.

Games:
8 June: Group A, Russia v Czech Republic
12 June: Group A, Greece v Czech Republic
16 June: Group A, Czech Republic v Poland

Ukraine

New Lviv Stadium

Club: FC Karpaty Lviv
UEFA Euro 2012 capacity: 30,000

Fans who went to UEFA Euro 2008 in Austria may think they have taken a wrong turning when they arrive in Lviv – this stadium was built on exactly the same design as the Euro 2008 venue in Klagenfurt! You'll find it on the outskirts of the city.

Games:
9 June: Group B, Germany v Portugal
13 June: Group B, Denmark v Portugal
17 June: Group B, Denmark v Germany

Olympic Stadium Kyiv

Club: None
UEFA Euro 2012 capacity: 60,000

This is the biggest stadium being used in UEFA Euro 2012, with a capacity of 60,000 – and it's where the final itself will be staged. Every player and fan will be hoping to end up here on 1 July and it should be a novel experience – the stadium is covered by a transparent roof!

Games:
11 June: Group stage, Ukraine v Sweden
15 June: Group D, Sweden v England
19 June: Group D, Sweden v France
24 June: Quarter-final 4
1 July: Final

Metalist Stadium

Club: FC Metalist Kharkiv
UEFA Euro 2012 capacity: 30,000

This famous old ground was first built in 1926 but nobody who attended games in those days would recognize it now! Local fans have nicknamed it the Spider Arena as the roof supports look like spider legs.

Games:
9 June: Group B, Netherlands v Denmark
13 June: Group B, Netherlands v Germany
17 June: Group B, Portugal v Netherlands

Donbass Arena

Club: FC Shakhtar Donetsk
UEFA Euro 2012 capacity: 50,000

The Donbass is only a few years old (it was opened in 2009) and its ultra-modern design was funded by Shakhtar Donetsk's super-rich owner Rinat Akhmetov. You may recognize it from UEFA Champions League fixtures and it features an illuminated exterior and infrared heating. At night a huge fountain built alongside the stadium lights up, topped by a 30-tonne football! A quarter-final and semi-final will be staged here.

Games:
11 June: Group D, France v England
15 June: Group D, Ukraine v France
19 June: Group D, England v Ukraine
23 June: Quarter-final 3
27 June: Semi-final 1

Rules of the Tournament

This will be the last UEFA Euro Finals to feature 16 teams – the 2016 event in France will see 24 take part.

In Ukraine and Poland the 16 teams will be split into four groups, with games in each group split between just two stadiums. Poland will play in Group A and Ukraine in Group D; a draw will be held to decide other placings.

The top two in each group move on to the quarter-finals (the winner of Group A faces the runner-up in Group B and so on) when the games become knockout matches – with the winner decided if necessary by extra time and penalties.

In the group stage, if teams finish on the same number of points, the team to go through will be determined in the following order:

1   The team with the higher number of points obtained against rivals on the same points total
2   The team with the superior goal difference in matches against the teams in question
3   The team with the most goals scored in matches against the teams in question
4   The team with superior goal difference in all group matches
5   Position in the UEFA national team coefficient ranking system
6   The team with the best fair play record in the tournament
7   The drawing of lots

There is one exception – if two teams which have the same number of points and also the same number of goals scored and conceded play their last group match against each other and are still equal at the end of that match, the ranking of the two teams in question is determined by penalties (as long as no other teams in the group are on the same points total).

There you go – simple! You got it, didn't you?

Euro 2012 City Guide

Euro 2012 aims to show off all that is good in the European footballing world, with the matches taking place in eight different cities – split equally between Poland and Ukraine. Here is a brief city-by-city guide for what players and spectators alike can expect to find away from the football.

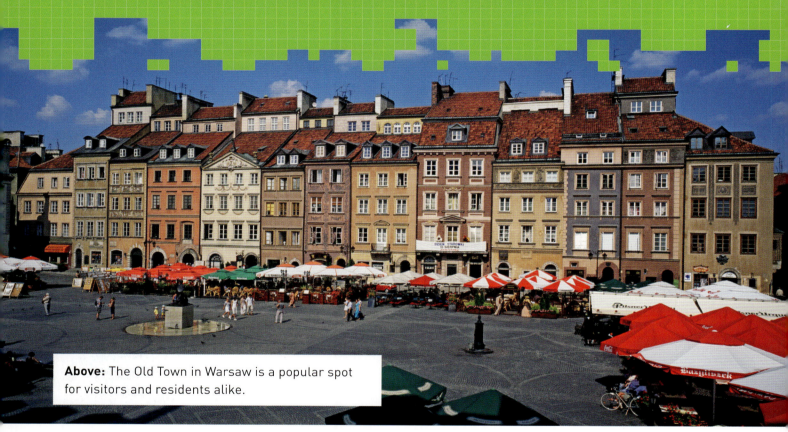

Above: The Old Town in Warsaw is a popular spot for visitors and residents alike.

Poland

Gdansk has only been part of Poland since 1945 but has played a huge part in its history, as it was here that "Solidarity", which led in part to the fall of communism, was born. Ulica Dluga and Dlugi Targ – Long Street and Long Market – are the main tourist attractions, and galleries and cafes on the waterfront are worth visiting.

Poznan's Old Town has barely changed since 1253, and should be the first port of call for any visitors to Poland's fifth-oldest city. There are a seemingly limitless number of trade fairs, part of the reason Poznan is second only to Warsaw in terms of importance to the Polish economy.

Warsaw is known as "the Phoenix City" – and for good reason. Almost one million people died during World War II as the city was heavily bombed, but the reconstruction of Poland's capital has ensured it is a thriving and vibrant city. The Old Town is on UNESCO's World Heritage List and there are countless museums and restaurants to keep visitors entertained.

Wroclaw is spread across 12 islands, linked by 112 bridges – and each island has a separate identity. The town hall is so big that it incorporates three internal streets and took almost 200 years to build, while the Raclawicka Panorama – a 114m-long panoramic painting housed in a rotunda – is the city's pride and joy.

Ukraine

Lviv has a coffee-house culture that is more akin to Hungary or Austria than Ukraine. It kept Ukrainian culture and language alive during occupation, with the Ploshcha Rynok – Market Square – the main tourist attraction.

Kharkiv is one of Ukraine's industrial centres. Ploshcha Svobody – Freedom Square – is the world's ninth-largest square and is the main hub for tourists.

Donetsk was only founded in 1869 as a steel mill and several coal mines were established in the area, but it is now recognized by UNESCO as the world's cleanest industrial city.

Kyiv was described as "the joy of the world" by medieval chroniclers. The largest city in Ukraine, and its business centre, Kyiv has recovered from the Nazi occupation 1941–43, and expanded after the city reclaimed land on the left bank of the Dnipro river – with led to the creation of many new beaches. With more than 100 museums, 33 theatres, 141 libraries, Khreshchatyk Street – the city's main artery – and St Andrew's Church there is plenty to keep the visitor occupied.

Henri Delaunay Trophy

Henri Delaunay was UEFA's first Secretary-General, and the man who first came up with the idea of a European Championship, having been partly responsible, along with Jules Rimet, for organizing the first World Cup.

Delaunay did not live to see his dream come to fruition, though, as he died in 1955, some five years before the first tournament. Yet his son, Pierre, became the driving force behind the European Nations Cup Committee, with the tournament initially named after his father as recognition for his contribution to European football.

Now only the trophy is named after the competition's founding father, although the current incarnation has only been in existence since 2008, when it was remodelled and made larger.

Left: The beautiful Henri Delaunay Trophy will be handed to the captain of the winners of the Euro 2012 final at the Kyiv Olympic Stadium on 1 July.

Euro 2012 Draw

Everyone is looking forward to the UEFA Euro 2012 tournament in Poland and Ukraine but before we could watch the stunning talents of Cristiano Ronaldo, David Silva and the rest, we needed to know which teams would face off against each other.

The drama began to unfold in Kyiv, the capital city of Ukraine, at the start of December and we had lots of drama to talk about as the draw paired some thrilling match-ups together.

But before Europe's finest knew who they would play, we were treated to a variety of dance acts, music and a "who's who" of European football, with legends such as Marco van Basten and Zinedine Zidane taking to the stage.

We even had the official unveiling of the tournament football – named the Tango 12 – to take in before the serious stuff began and the seeding of the groups. As Euro 2012 is hosted in Poland and Ukraine, the two countries got to be seeded first and they were then joined by Europe's heavyweights Spain and Holland as the first names in the other groups.

All the big names were there in Kyiv, with UEFA president Michel Platini keeping a close eye on the draw too – and what a draw it was, with some massive ties in the group stages for everyone to get excited about.

There was enough time for the Czech Republic to get drawn in Poland's Group A and Denmark to make their way into Holland's Group B before some real drama – Republic of Ireland landed in Group C along with holders Spain! It was a massive moment for Giovanni Trapattoni's men, who last played at a major tournament at the FIFA World Cup in 2002.

As the action unfolded at the glitzy ceremony in Kiev it was clear to see that all eyes were on Group B, with Denmark and Holland joined by Germany and Portugal as a frightening "Group of Death". What a group it promises to be, with Ronaldo going up against the likes of Arjen

Left: The draw for the finals has become an event in its own right and the Ukraine organizers didn't disappoint.

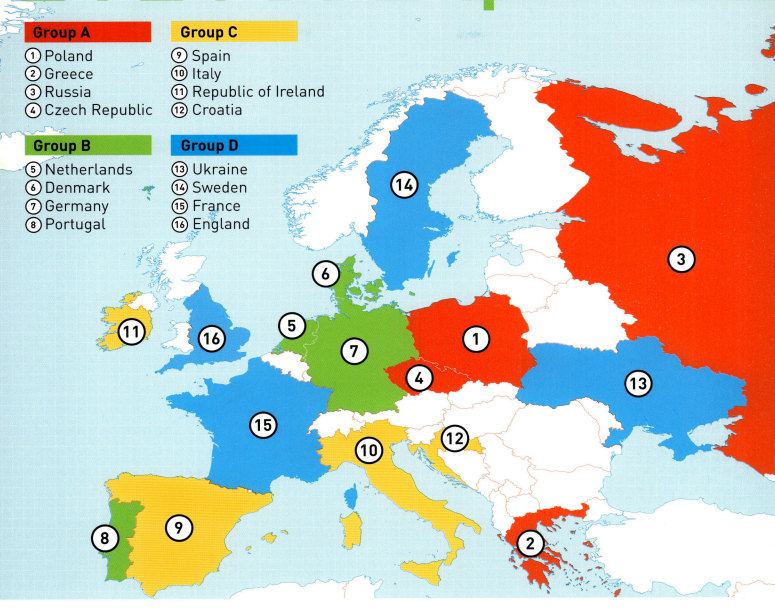

Group A
① Poland
② Greece
③ Russia
④ Czech Republic

Group C
⑨ Spain
⑩ Italy
⑪ Republic of Ireland
⑫ Croatia

Group B
⑤ Netherlands
⑥ Denmark
⑦ Germany
⑧ Portugal

Group D
⑬ Ukraine
⑭ Sweden
⑮ France
⑯ England

Robben, Christian Eriksen and Mesut Ozil.

England fans had a long wait until they found out who the Three Lions would face next summer as they were the last team drawn out of the hat. Fabio Capello's men were drawn into Group D against France, Ukraine and Sweden and it was a kind draw for England as they could have been in the same group as Spain and Italy or Portugal and Germany.

The draw has got everyone eagerly awaiting the start of the tournament and Euro 2012 kicks off with a cracking weekend of games. Joint hosts Poland tackle Greece on Saturday 8 June, followed by Russia versus the Czech Republic and the day after there's a massive double-header as Holland face Denmark before Germany take on Portugal.

Having seen each team's group and the sides they have to face, thoughts immediately turned to the real action on the field in the summer and what a tournament it promises to be.

Poland
Dreaming of glory

Poland have a proud football history and their current team are hoping to create waves too – especially as they are co-hosts of UEFA Euro 2012 and will be able to play their first round group matches in their home stadiums in front of their own fans.

Perhaps the most famous Polish team of all time was the one that qualified for the World Cup Finals of 1974 by holding England to a draw at Wembley. The Poles finished third in the finals, with striker Grzegorz Lato winning the Golden Boot after scoring seven goals.

Poland also finished third in the World Cup of 1982, beating France in the third-place play-off match. So what can they achieve on home soil in UEFA Euro 2012?

Expectations in Poland are being kept as low as possible, because fans have suffered many years of disappointment since 1982.

There was reason for optimism for Poland when they qualified for Euro 2008 – their first ever European Championships – finishing above Portugal in their qualifying group. But the finals didn't go the way they had hoped, losing to Germany in the first game, then drawing with co-hosts Austria before losing

Above: Poland have played more than 20 friendlies in the past two years as they prepare for Euro 2012.

1–0 to Croatia and thus being knocked out at the group stage.

The 2010 World Cup qualifiers went badly, as they finished fifth in their group. And there have been no qualifying games since they qualified for Euro 2012 as co-hosts.

So how will they do? That's a big question and one every fan in Poland is asking. They may not win the tournament, but they certainly won't be pushovers. Playing at home is a huge advantage in a tournament and some recent results in friendlies have given room for optimism, especially a 2–1 defeat of Argentina in the new national stadium in Warsaw.

Poland will be tough to score against because they have some top goalkeepers, such as Arsenal's Wojciech Szczesny and Lucasz Fabianski, former Celtic No. 1 Artur Boruc and Tomasz Kuszczak, once of Manchester United.

Borussia Dortmund midfielder Jakub Blaszczykowski, Poland's captain, will have to be influential. But their hopes may depend on the form of strikers Robert Lewandowski, also of Dortmund, Pawel Brozek of Trabzonspor and Euzebiusz Smolarek, who scored nine goals in qualifying for Euro 2008 but has played little since.

Right: Poland need Robert Lewandowski (9) to score goals at Euro 2012.

Ones to watch

Jakub Blaszczykowski

Many Poles believe UEFA Euro 2012 will be the stage that turns Blaszczykowski into a world star. The 25-year-old Borussia Dortmund man, who plays with "Kuba" on his back in Germany, has been growing in stature over recent years and now looks potentially Poland's best player. He provides real skill, pace and trickery on the wing and has been voted Poland and Dortmund player of the year in his career so far. He could be one that really entertains crowds when the tournament gets underway – and, having missed UEFA Euro 2008 through injury, he will be highly motivated to shine this time.

Meet the coach

Franciszek Smuda

The experienced Smuda has been in charge of Poland since 2009 and is highly respected in his home country both as a coach and as a player. Now aged 63, he played club football in Poland, the United States and Germany and won three Polish League titles as a coach (with Widzew Lodz and Wisla Krakow) as well as the Polish Cup with Lech Poznan before taking over the national team. He guided his side to the UEFA Euro 2008 Finals.

Russia
Credible threat again

Semi-finalists in 2008, Russia will be hoping to go one better this time around and win their first European Championship. Although they can claim to have won it in a different guise in 1960, when they were part of the former Soviet Union. No other country can say they have done that!

When the European Championships started in 1960, Russia was a part of the Soviet Union, and the USSR won the inaugural tournament, beating Yugoslavia 2–1 in the final.

Independent Russia played its first friendly in 1992, winning 2–0 against Mexico. Since then Russia has gone on to become one of the more dangerous teams in international football. However, they haven't enjoyed much success in the European Championships.

In four attempts, they have advanced from the group stage only once, in 2008, when they beat one of the favourites, the Netherlands, in the quarter-finals before losing to eventual winners Spain in the last four.

In qualifying for Euro 2012, Russia were undefeated away from home, winning four times and drawing once. Their defence was outstanding, conceding just four goals in 10 matches, while they netted 17 at the other end.

Above: Russia haven't enjoyed the European Championship glory of the old Soviet Union, but Euro 2012 may be different.

Right: Vasili Berezutski (3) is a solid defender for Russia.

They will be one of the dark horses when it comes to winning the tournament but manager Dick Advocaat will have a plan to make sure his team reaches the latter stages and the other nations would be silly to underestimate them.

Russia have a mix of experienced players such as Yuri Zhirkov and captain Andrey Arshavin, not to mention talented youngsters such as Alan Dzagoev.

Also key to them succeeding in Poland–Ukraine will be striker Roman Pavlyuchenko. He is closing in on becoming Russia's all-time leading goalscorer – Vladimir Beschastnykh currently holds the record with 26 goals in 71 appearances. Pavlyuchenko was on 20 goals from 45 games by the time they qualified for Euro 2012. It is fair to say he could even break that record in Poland–Ukraine if Russia have a decent run.

And in goalkeeper Igor Akinfeev, they have one of the best shot-stoppers in Europe. He has also been named Russian goalkeeper of the year six times, the latest coming in 2010. That's some achievement considering he was only 24 at the time.

Although not one of the favourites, Russia have plenty of talent to trouble most teams and will be hoping that they can win their first trophy since gaining independence!

One to watch

Andrey Arshavin

The 2006 Russian footballer of the year, his performances at the European 2008 Championship made him a star. He was selected in the team of the tournament and he will be hoping to repeat that feat in Poland–Ukraine. Those displays also prompted a big-money move to Arsenal and the Premier League. The attacking midfielder is known for his ability to set up goals as well as getting on the scoresheet himself. When he does score, he often celebrates by pulling a funny face or putting his finger on his lips to silence the crowd.

Meet the coach

Dick Advocaat

Nicknamed "The Little General", manager Dick Advocaat is very experienced when it comes to leading teams to glory, as his record at club level suggests. Having won the Dutch league with PSV Eindhoven, the Scottish league twice with Rangers and the Russian league with Zenit Saint Petersburg, Advocaat is definitely a winner. And he is also known for winning cup competitions, something he proved when winning the UEFA Cup and UEFA Super Cup with Zenit. His track record in knockout competitions will prove to be useful when he arrives in Poland–Ukraine and Russia are definitely a threat with him in charge.

Greece
Underdogs who can bite

Surprise winners of Euro 2004 in Portugal, in only their third appearance in a major competition, the Greeks will go into this tournament as clear outsiders despite their heroic display eight years ago. They have since qualified two more times for the finals but never progressed to the knockout stages.

Above: Shock winners in 2004, Greece probably will never creep up on rivals with bigger reputations again.

Greece are often accused of playing physical, defensive, boring football – yet those were the key points behind their Euro success in the past. That and a killer attacking instinct up front – similar to an Italian-style Catenaccio, just more frustrating to watch.

But make no mistake. Their team work-rate is higher than most. Greece might not have many superstars, but they give everything for each other and their midfield possesses invaluable experience. The likes of Kostas Katsouranis and Giorgos Karagounis know what it's like to succeed and, with almost 200 caps between them, they will prove to be a tough team to beat.

Up front, look out for Greece's hero Angelos Charisteas, a striker blessed with a talent for scoring the most important goals for the team, including the Euro 2004 winner. Together, he and the technically gifted Georgos Samaras should command respect from opponents.

Ultimately the nation's eyes will be on the manager should the team fail to achieve their targets. Fernando Santos, the 57-year-old Portuguese, known as "The Engineer", has some big shoes to fill. After all, previous manager Otto Rehhagel only guided the team to Championship glory!

The team have lost some of their most experienced players in recent years, with defender Theodoros Zagorakis, striker Angelos Basinas and legendary goalkeeper Antonios Nikopolidis all retiring. Santos will have to find the balance quickly between the remaining old guard and a growing number of outstanding young prospects available.

Schalke central defender Kyriakos Papadopoulos was only 19 when Greece qualified, but he is highly regarded and considered "the next Zagorakis". Together with young striker Stefanos Athanasiadis he will be looking to make an instant impact on these finals.

But there is one player who stands out more than all the others: Sotiris Ninis. When the 21-year-old is fit, he is top-class. Skilful, with pace and with sublime vision and fearsome shooting skills, Ninis can be unpredictable. He is also Greece's youngest-ever scorer, with a goal on his debut at just 18 years of age.

Left: Can "The Engineer" build another winning team with Greece?

One to watch

Giorgos Karagounis

Giorgos Karagounis is best remembered for a long-range goal against Portugal in the opening match of Euro 2004. It will be his responsibility to guide the team after the departure of Angelos Basinas and Theodoros Zagorakis. He is short but built like a tank. To that he adds incredible technique and a fearsome shot. Currently playing for Panathinaikos, where he launched his career before spells with Benfica and Inter Milan, he has over 100 caps for his country. As captain, he led the Greek national team to its first win in a World Cup match with a 2–1 win against Nigeria in 2010.

Meet the coach

Fernando Santos

Fernando Santos, 57, has coached some of the biggest clubs in Greece and his native Portugal. In February 2010, as part of the Greek league's 50th anniversary celebrations, he was selected as the best coach of the decade. Greece is his first international job, but his impact has been tremendous. His team went undefeated in his first 16 games, including 10 wins. Greece won their qualifying group, ahead of Croatia and Israel with seven wins in 10 matches, and just five goals conceded.

Czech Republic
Punching above its weight

The Czech Republic regularly produces talented players – and they have enjoyed great success at the UEFA European Championships. As Czechoslovakia, they won the tournament in 1976 and in 1996 they reached the final. This summer, they want to experience more of those glory days.

The Czech Republic love the European Championship. Ever since the country split from Slovakia in 1993, they have qualified for every tournament. Plus, if you include their record as Czechoslovakia, they have reached two finals, winning one, and have also reached the semi-finals three times. The last time they did this was in 2004, when they were beaten by eventual champions Greece. In that tournament, Czech striker Milan Baros was the competition's top scorer with five goals.

This success has been possible because of the quality of their players. They have a long history of producing technically gifted midfielders capable of playing for Europe's biggest clubs. Karel Poborsky was a superb winger with bags of tricks who spent some of his career with Manchester United, Benfica and Lazio.

Then there was Vladimir Smicer, the former Liverpool attacking midfielder who scored a great goal in the 2005 Champions League

Above: The Czech Republic have surprised fans at previous European Championships, and they can do it again in 2012.

Right: Will Tomas Rosicky, "Little Mozart", be the Czech's maestro?

final. However, the best of them all was probably former Juventus and Lazio player Pavel Nedved, who was one of the world's best midfielders during the late 1990s and early 2000s.

Skipper Tomas Rosicky is the modern player most like these former greats, even though, at 31, he might be a little past his best. Now it is up to young stars, such as Vaclav Pilar, to provide the team with creativity.

Unlike in previous years, though, the Czech Republic look stronger at the back than they do going forward. Chelsea goalkeeper Petr Cech is one of the world's best, and defenders such as Michal Kadlec, Tomas Sivok and Daniel Pudil all have many international caps despite being only in their mid-20s.

Up front, there is also some emerging new talent. Even though experienced striker Milan Baros is still around, youngsters Tomas Necid and Tomas Pekhart will be hoping to make an impact at this tournament.

The Czechs were not impressive in qualifying. They lost three matches – albeit two to the mighty Spain – and sneaked into the play-offs as Group I runners-up. However, they then produced good performances to beat Montenegro in the play-off, winning 2–0 at home, then triumphing 1–0 in the away leg.

One to watch

Tomas Rosicky

Tomas Rosicky remains one of the most technically gifted players in Europe. The former Borussia Dortmund playmaker, nicknamed "Little Mozart", moved to Arsenal in 2006 and quickly established himself as one of Arsene Wenger's key men. A horrible run of injuries, which started in 2009, has really affected him, but he remains a crucial part of the Czech Republic team even at the age of 31. He missed only one game in the qualifiers, providing four assists for his team, and will aim to maintain these sorts of standards during the European Championships.

Meet the coach

Michal Bilek

Michal Bilek has been the Czech Republic coach since 2009, ending a run of three national managers in 12 months. As a player, he spent most of his career at Sparta Prague, with four separate spells there. He also played for Real Betis in Spain. A midfielder who could also play at right-back, with Sparta Prague he won three league and two Czechoslovakian cups. He coached in Costa Rica before returning home and winning the double with Sparta Prague. He was first appointed the national team's assistant coach, but was promoted when manager Ivan Hasek became the Czech FA's president.

Group A: Euro Stars

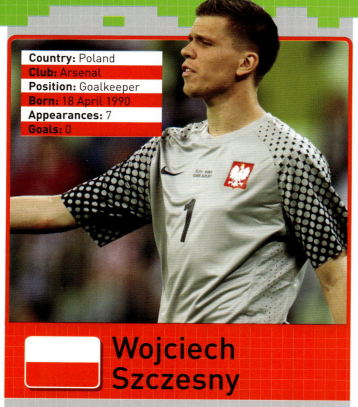

Country: Poland
Club: Arsenal
Position: Goalkeeper
Born: 18 April 1990
Appearances: 7
Goals: 0

Wojciech Szczesny

Skills and Strengths

Most goalkeepers don't get the number one jersey until they are in their late 20s but Wojciech Szczesny isn't most goalkeepers. At 21 he has the presence of a 31-year-old and stands tall at 6'5". He can be seen shouting at defenders and telling them what to do, despite being one of the youngest players on the pitch. His excellent shot-stopping abilities and commanding authority have even drawn praise from German legend Oliver Kahn, when the two nations met during a friendly and the match finished 2–2. The son of former Poland goalkeeper Maciej Szczesny, he has a brother, Jan, who is also a professional goalkeeper, so it seems that being a goalkeeper runs in the Szczesny family.

Goals and Glory

With club team Arsenal, he won the FA Youth Cup in 2009 and the Premier Academy League the same year. He also played in the 2011 Carling Cup final when Arsenal lost 2–1 to Birmingham.

Claim to Fame

He saved a vital penalty in Arsenal's UEFA Champions League qualifying game against Udinese, which the Gunners went on to win 3–1 on aggregate and qualify for the group stages of the competition.

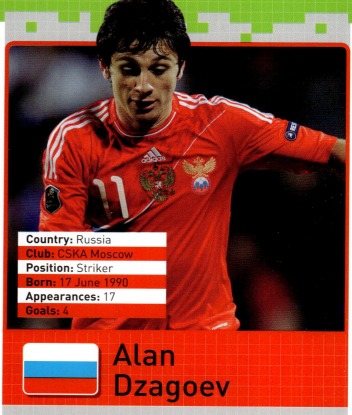

Country: Russia
Club: CSKA Moscow
Position: Striker
Born: 17 June 1990
Appearances: 17
Goals: 4

Alan Dzagoev

Skills and Strengths

Described as the most talented footballer in Russia by captain Andrey Arshavin, Alan Dzagoev is certainly one to watch at the European Championships. His ability to find space in the tightest of gaps makes him extremely difficult to mark. Add to that his speed and his ability in the air and Russia have one of the hottest prospects in world football at the moment. And, given that he is still only 21, he clearly has a lot to offer football over the next few years. With him pulling the strings for his country, he will have many defenders worried as he lines up against them.

Goals and Glory

With club CSKA Moscow, Dzagoev has won the Russian cup three times (in 2008, 2009 and 2011) as well as the Russian super cup once (in 2009).

Claim to Fame

In 2008 he was voted Best Young Player in the Russian Premier League in his debut season for CSKA Moscow. Later that year, he became the youngest outfield player to appear for Russia when he came on as a substitute against Germany in a World Cup qualifier and his first goal came against the Republic of Ireland in October 2010. He is definitely a star for the future.

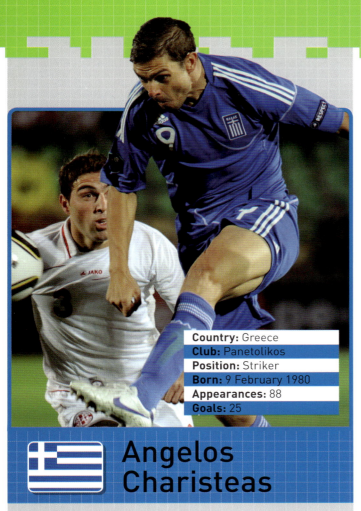

Country: Greece
Club: Panetolikos
Position: Striker
Born: 9 February 1980
Appearances: 88
Goals: 25

Angelos Charisteas

Skills and Strengths

At 31, this could be Angelos Charisteas's last major international tournament – but he will be forever remembered by fans in Greece for his contribution to the national's team glorious run to win the 2004 European Championship. He scored three goals in the tournament, including the only goal in the quarter-final against France, and the one which won the final. Entering 2012, he is five goals away from becoming Greece's all-time top scorer, an accolade currently held by the retired Nikos Anastopoulos. A predator in the penalty area, Charisteas is a real threat in the air as well as with his feet, and will be hoping to once again fire his nation to European success.

Goals and Glory

Charisteas won the German domestic double with Werder Bremen in 2004, the Dutch cup double with Ajax in 2006 and the German cup with Schalke in 2004. He was also a key member of the Greek squad that won Euro 2004 in Portugal.

Claim to Fame

He scored the winning goal in the final of Euro 2004 to beat Portugal 1–0 and was named in the UEFA team of the tournament.

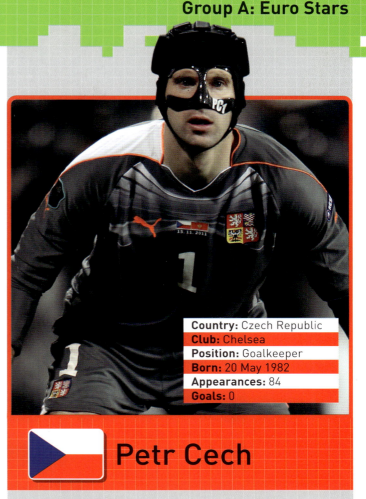

Country: Czech Republic
Club: Chelsea
Position: Goalkeeper
Born: 20 May 1982
Appearances: 84
Goals: 0

Petr Cech

Skills and Strengths

Cech, a commanding 6'6" tall, has been one of the best goalkeepers in the world for nearly a decade for both Chelsea and the Czech Republic. Agile for a big man, he is capable of making saves that many smaller goalkeepers can't. He is also a good leader and, having been his country's number-one keeper for nearly 10 years, is well respected and trusted by team-mates.

Goals and Glory

With Chelsea, Cech has won almost every honour in English football. Although Claudio Rainieri was Blues manager when Cech signed the contract in February 2004, his Chelsea debut came under the managership of Jose Mourinho. At Stamford Bridge, Cech has won the Premier League and FA Cup three times each, and was a Champions League runner-up in 2008. He was a European Under-21 Championship winner in 2002.

Claim to Fame

Cech has been named the Czech Republic's player of the year four times, UEFA's best goalkeeper twice and Chelsea's player of the year in 2011. In 2006, he suffered a serious head injury playing for Chelsea and now wears protective headgear in every match.

Netherlands
Dutch masters return

The Netherlands have a fantastic record in this competition. They have reached the quarter-finals twice, semi-finals three times and the one time they reached the final they won it. They love the European Championships and the way they play exciting football, the European Championship loves them.

Above: The Netherlands won their first nine matches in qualifying for Euro 2012.

Nicknamed "Oranjie", *the Orange*, the Netherlands were the creators of "total football" which was led by star player Johan Cruyff and manager Rinus Michels. The philosophy has continued ever since, and has seen them become one of the world's best teams. They can pass the ball around teams as if they weren't even on the pitch and their opponents regularly struggle to regain the ball after losing possession.

When they won the European Championship in West Germany in 1988, they knocked out the hosts 2–1 in the semi-finals and beat the Soviet Union in the final 2–0. They were the fourth team to qualify for Euro 2012 and won nine of their 10 qualifying games, including an impressive 11–0 victory over San Marino, their biggest in history!

The team boasts outstanding attacking players, such as Wesley Sneijder, Robin van Persie, Rafael van der Vaart and Arjen Robben. And having tough tacklers such as Nigel de Jong and Mark van Bommel in the midfield, the defence often has very little to do for long periods of the match.

The retirement of goalkeeper Edwin van der Sar has not weakened the team as they have Maarten Stekelenburg as the current number one and his understudy, 23-year-old Tim Krul, likely to push Stekelenburg for the Dutch goalkeeping shirt over the next few years.

And do not forget that they can call upon the experienced Ruud van Nistelrooy to help them out. Age doesn't seem to stop this striker from scoring and he is closing in on the all-time Dutch national goalscoring record, currently held by Patrick Kluivert with 40 goals. Remember that in case you're ever asked that in a quiz.

With so much talent to choose from, coach Bert van Marwijk will have a difficult time narrowing the numbers to 23. But whichever players he does pick, be sure to see them in the later rounds of the tournament. And, if all goes well, they may just lift the Henri Delaunay Trophy come 1 July.

Right:
Bert van Marwijk has a wealth of talent to choose from.

Ones to watch

Mark van Bommel
Dutch footballer of the year in 2001 and 2005, captain Mark van Bommel has won over 70 caps for his country and scored 10 goals. Not bad for a defensive midfielder. He was made captain by his father-in-law Bert van Marwijk and led the team in their 5-0 victory over San Marino. So far it seems this father–son-in-law partnership is working well and van Bommel is relishing the role of a leader on the pitch. A tough-tackling player, he has enjoyed success with Fortuna Sittard, PSV Eindhoven, Barcelona, Bayern Munich and most recently Inter Milan.

Meet the coach

Bert van Marwijk
Bert van Marwijk rarely loses as Dutch national coach, but one loss came against Spain in the 2010 World Cup final. As a player, he won only one cap for his country, but van Marwijk succeeded legendary ex-star Marco van Basten as national coach after Euro 2008. His team plays the free-flowing style of football for which the Dutch are famous and after his first 40 games in charge, they had scored 91 goals! The other 15 teams at Euro 2012 had better beware.

Germany
Three-times champions

When it comes to European Championships, Germany is the daddy of them of all! The Germans have won three times (more than any other country), lifting the trophy in 1972, 1980 and 1996 – and they are one of the big favourites for UEFA Euro 2012 too.

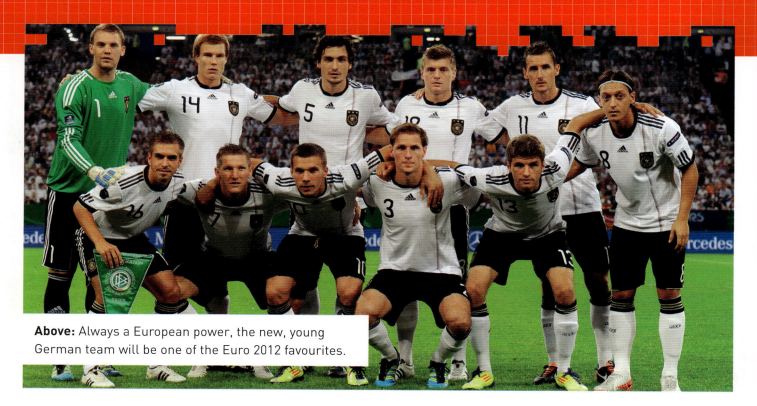

Above: Always a European power, the new, young German team will be one of the Euro 2012 favourites.

What can you say about Germany that we don't already know? They never miss a penalty, never give up until the very last second of a match, always qualify with ease and always perform at major finals once they get there. They are a mean, lean footballing machine!

Don't expect it to be any different this time, either, because the new-look Germany under coach Joachim Low are as good as ever and will surely be one of the favourites. Let's look at the evidence in their favour.

First of all it's worth knowing that apart from Germany only Spain and France have won more than one European Championship. So you can see that the Germans – who already have three – are way ahead of most of their rivals, having also qual fied for every Finals since 1972. Add in the fac: that Germany have won three World Cups and you realize why they have long been regarded as a football superpower.

They are no slouches these days, either, having been the first team to qualify for UEFA

Euro 2012 – winning all 10 qualifying matches and scoring 34 goals in the process. Basically, if you have Germany in Top Trumps, you are holding one seriously powerful card!

The current team is packed with exciting young players such as Bayern Munich's attacking midfielder Thomas Muller (the Golden Boot winner at the World Cup 2010), winger Lukas Podolski, wonderkid midfielder Mario Goetz, Real Madrid star Sami Khedira and goalkeeper Manuel Neuer.

Their recent record, even during a rebuilding period, is hugely impressive because Germany reached the semi-finals of the last World Cup and the final of the Euro 2008. On both occasions they lost to champions Spain – and this time the Germans believe they can get even closer to Andres Iniesta and co.

They won't lack experience either. Striker Miroslav Klose has won more than 100 caps and scored more than 60 goals; and former captain Michael Ballack is still available if required.

The good news for fans, too, is that under head coach Joachim Low, Germany play an exciting attacking game; adding flair and ambition to their athleticism and mental strength. That's a powerful combination – so look out for Germany in Poland and Ukraine!

Left: Joachim Low is one of the few German national coaches not to have been a star player.

One to watch

Philipp Lahm

The ever-reliable Lahm replaced legendary midfielder Michael Ballack as captain of Germany, which is quite a task. But, as one of the world's best full-backs, who has played in four major tournaments since making his debut in 2004, he has taken it in his stride.

Lahm, who is still only 27 years old, was particularly impressive at UEFA Euro 2008 and in the World Cup Finals of 2010 in South Africa – where he was the only player in the Germany team to play every single minute of their campaign. He often plays at left-back, even though he is right-footed.

Meet the coach

Joachim Low

Joachim Low, nicknamed Jogi, is 51 years old and has transformed Germany since taking over from Jurgen Klinsmann in 2006, turning the Germans into a real attacking force. Formerly Klinsmann's assistant, he really came into his own when given the big job – guiding Germany to the final of UEFA Euro 2008, where they lost narrowly to Spain, and taking the World Cup Finals by storm in 2010, thrashing both England and Argentina before losing in the last four.

Portugal
Mercurial brilliance

Portugal, despite being able to call on many talented players over the years, have never won the European Championship, but they often have come close. In 2004, on home soil, they were beaten in the final by Greece, and they reached the semi-finals in 1984 and 2000. Is this finally their year?

Over the years Portugal have fielded some of football's greats, from the legendary Eusebio through to Luis Figo and current world star Cristiano Ronaldo. Their history in the Euros is mixed – their first finals appearance was only in 1984, but they did reach the last four, losing 3–2 to winners France after extra time.

The next time they qualified was in 1996, but eventual runners-up the Czech Republic beat them in the quarter-final. France again did for them in a dramatic semi-final at Euro 2000, again after extra time, with Zinedine Zidane scoring a late Silver Goal penalty to give them a 2–1 win.

Portugal hosted Euro 2004, but were foiled by unfashionable Greece, who beat them in both the opening match and the final. Greece's defensive style of play won them few friends, while Portugal tried to play expressive, flowing football, but in the end

Above: Portugal have a difficult task to reach the last eight with the Netherlands and Germany in their group.

Right: Cristiano Ronaldo is one of the greatest players ever to represent Portugal.

could not break down their opponents. Euro 2008 held still more disappointment, when they were knocked out by runners-up Germany in the quarter-final.

Portugal qualified for Euro 2012 via the play-offs, beating Bosnia 6–2 at home after a goalless draw in the away leg. Captain and star player Cristiano Ronaldo scored twice as they ultimately made their way to the tournament in style. Their attack is their best attribute – Portugal scored 21 goals in just eight group qualifying matches, though they still finished second to Denmark.

Their current crop of players are some of the most talented footballers around, including Ronaldo, who many people think rivals Lionel Messi as the best player in the world. He is third on Portugal's all-time scorers' list, level with Luis Figo on 32 goals. Pauleta and Eusebio are first and second, with 47 and 41.

Other important players for Portugal include winger Nani and midfielders Joao Moutinho and Raul Meireles, as well as defenders Pepe and Bruno Alves – not that much of Portugal's focus is on defensive play. With such a dazzling array of attacking options available, Portugal will be a team to watch at Euro 2012!

One to watch

Cristiano Ronaldo

Cristiano Ronaldo became the most expensive player in football history at £80 million when he moved from Manchester United to Real Madrid in 2009 and has not stopped scoring goals since. He is also one of the most recognizable footballers in the world. He captained his country for the first time after his 22nd birthday in 2007, under Luiz Felipe Scolari. Carlos Queiroz and Paulo Bento, the next Portugal coaches, have also made Ronaldo captain. The supremely confident maestro will be sure he can lead Portugal to Euro 2012 victory.

Meet the coach

Paul Bento

Coach Paulo Bento is relatively inexperienced, having only previously taken charge of Sporting Lisbon in his short managerial career. But it was then that players such as Nani and Miguel Veloso broke through, and he broke several club records while in charge. These included back-to-back Portuguese cups for the first time since 1974, and he made it the first time since 1962 that Sporting finished in the top two in the league in consecutive seasons. He was appointed Portugal manager in September 2010 and justified the choice by steering the team to Euro 2012.

Denmark
The Olsen Gang

Denmark won the European Championship for the first and only time in 1992. Now nicknamed "the Olsen Gang", after long-serving manager Morten Olsen, they have a largely youthful squad. Winning the competition will be tough – but if they can make it to the knockout stages, anything can happen.

Above: Having qualified for Euro 2012 ahead of Portugal, everyone will take Denmark seriously.

Denmark enjoyed their most successful period in this competition in the early 1990s. With one of the best goalkeepers of all time in Peter Schmeichel, and the legendary Brian Laudrup leading from the front, they won Euro 1992 with an extremely tight defence and the ability to score in tense situations.

Beating Germany, the reigning 1990 World Cup winners, 2–0 in the final has so far been the high point of Danish footballing history, but many see the current team as one that can recapture some of that glory.

Their success in 1992 was based on a very strong defence. After their victory, it seemed many wanted a more attacking team to push on, but the team failed to live up to fans' expectations and couldn't make it past the group stage in 1996 and 2000.

Things improved in 2004 when they reached the quarter-final. They finished above Italy in the group stages – something not many teams can say they have done over the past few decades! In the quarter-finals Denmark met the Czech Republic and were unfortunately – for them – soundly beaten 3–0, but they put up a fight and were unlucky not to open the scoring in the first half.

They did not qualify for Euro 2008 and qualification for 2012 looked difficult with Portugal and Norway in their group. They got off to a good start, with four wins in their first six games, including two over Norway. Going into the final game, they were level on points with leaders Portugal.

As Portugal had beaten them 3–1 in Porto, a point would have given them automatic qualification. But manager Olsen had a few tricks up his sleeve and goals from Michael Krohn-Dehli and Nicklas Bendtner saw the Danes win 2–1 and qualify at Portugal's expense. Defender Simon Kjaer, midfielder Christian Eriksen and striker Bendtner are hot talents and will be the ones to watch as Denmark look to win their first trophy in 20 years.

Left: Morten Olsen has seen it all as a player and manager of Denmark.

One to watch

Thomas Sorensen

At 35, goalkeeper Thomas Sorensen is in the top 10 capped players in Denmark history. Seen as the successor to Peter Schmeichel, he gained his first international cap by replacing Schmeichel in a Euro 2000 qualifying game against Israel – a match Denmark won 3–0. Sorensen was the reserve goalkeeper for the 2000 tournament and took over from the Great Dane for the 2002 World Cup qualifying campaign. He was then a regular in the starting line-up and at Euro 2004 he was named man of the match in the group games against Italy and Bulgaria, keeping clean sheets in both.

Meet the coach

Morten Olsen

The only Danish man to reach 100 national matches as player and coach, Morten Olsen has been in charge of the side for 11 years! He also captained Denmark at three major tournaments and was the first Dane to reach 100 caps. He has taken his country to four major tournaments and, after qualifying for Euro 2012, the Danish FA want him to stay on past the finals. He is made for the Denmark national side ... even his glasses are Danish red!

Group B: Euro Stars

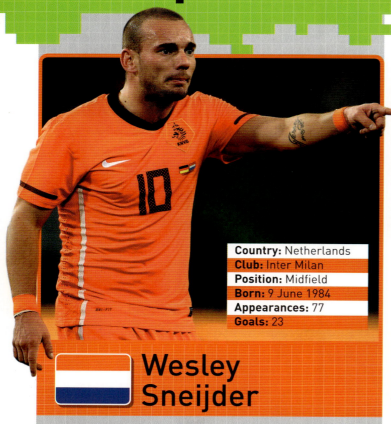

Country:	Netherlands
Club:	Inter Milan
Position:	Midfield
Born:	9 June 1984
Appearances:	77
Goals:	23

Wesley Sneijder

Skills and Strengths
Playmaker Wesley Sneijder is one of the most creative midfielders in modern football. He has an eye for finding a team-mate when the pass doesn't look possible, as well as scoring remarkable long-range goals. Whether it is assisting or scoring, he makes the extraordinary look ordinary!

Goals and Glory
Sneijder was part of the Inter Milan team that won five trophies in 2010 under Jose Mourinho – the Italian league, cup and super cup treble, UEFA Champions League and FIFA World Club Cup. He has also won the league titles in Spain, with Real Madrid, and at home, with Ajax. He scored two goals at Euro 2008 and five at the 2010 World Cup, where he helped the Netherlands reach the final, although they lost 1–0 Spain. It all goes to prove that Sneijder knows what it takes to score and succeed in major international tournaments.

Claim to Fame
Named in the Euro 2008 team of the tournament as well as winning the award for scoring the goal of the tournament, Sneijder also won the UEFA midfielder of the year in 2010 and, in the same year, was also voted in the UEFA team of the year.

Country:	Germany
Club:	Bayern Munich
Position:	Midfielder/striker
Born:	13 September 1989
Appearances:	25
Goals:	10

Thomas Muller

Skills and Strengths
Young star Muller – an attacking midfielder or striker – was one of the heroes of the 2010 World Cup in South Africa, bursting on to the scene with some incredible performances. His pace, power and finishing – not to mention his amazing energy – typified a new vibrant Germany side that crushed England 4–1 in a match where he scored two of the goals, and he opened the scoring when they whipped Argentina 4–0 in the knockout stages. He has already shown he is ready for the big stage despite his young age – his first goal for his country was at the 2010 World Cup.

Goals and Glory
2010 was a great year for Muller, who won the German league, cup and super cup with Bayern Munich, as well as a runners-up medal in the Champions League. On the international scene, he picked up a bronze medal as Germany won the third-place play-off at the FIFA 2010 World Cup in South Africa. It is difficult for a player to have a much better year than that!

Claim to Fame
Muller won not only the World Cup Golden Boot, with five goals and three assists, but he also received the award for the best young player at the tournament.

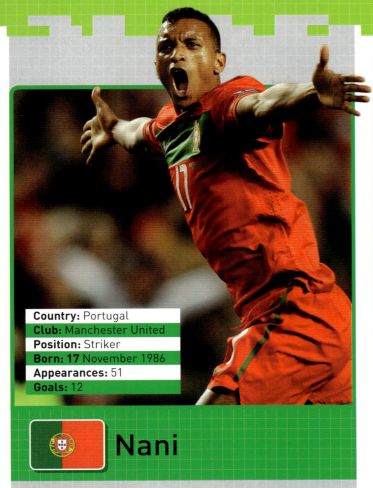

Country:	Portugal
Club:	Manchester United
Position:	Striker
Born:	**17** November 1986
Appearances:	51
Goals:	12

Nani

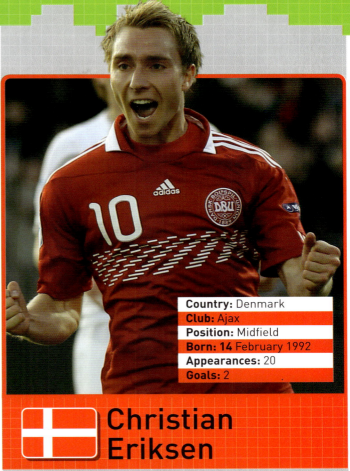

Country:	Denmark
Club:	Ajax
Position:	Midfield
Born:	**14** February 1992
Appearances:	20
Goals:	2

Christian Eriksen

Skills and Strengths

Although captain Cristiano Ronaldo receives all the plaudits, this is a chance for winger Nani to emerge from his shadow, just as he has done at Manchester United. Over the past few seasons the winger's performances, goal and assist tallies and recognition among fans and critics alike have been improving and increasing. With a marvellous ability to strike the ball from distance, hit swerving free kicks and twist the blood of opposition defenders with his quick feet, Nani looks sure to be a star at EURO 2012.

Goals and Glory

Nani has picked up three Premier League titles while at Manchester United (from 2007–08 to 2009–10) along with a League Cup (2008–09), although the FA Cup has escaped his grasp so far. He also collected a UEFA Champions League winner's medal in 2007–08 when he helped United beat Chelsea on penalties in the final in Moscow, and Nani was successful with his attempt.

Claim to Fame

Since Cristiano Ronaldo left Manchester United in 2009, Nani has come into his own. He was chosen in the PFA Premier League team of the year and was selected as the PFA player of the year in 2010–11.

Skills and Strengths

He is such an important player to Denmark's team that Christian Eriksen didn't play a single game at under-21 level before being selected for the national side at the age of 19 in March 2010. Despite his young age, he is already a key player for Denmark and his dribbling and passing ability has impressed many experts. That list includes Rio Ferdinand, who went on social networking site Twitter to say how amazing and talented he had been during England's 2–1 friendly defeat of Denmark at Copenhagen in February 2011. In a very unusual step, after more than a dozen appearances for the national team, Eriksen was selected to make his Danish under-21 debut in the 2011 European Championships.

Goals and Glory

Eriksen was a key contributor as Ajax won their first Dutch league championship in seven years in 2011. He scored six goals in 26 Eredivisie appearances for them that season.

Claim to Fame

In 2008, Eriksen won the Danish under-17 talent of the year and in 2011 scooped up the Ajax talent of the year as well as the Dutch young player of the year.

Spain
The ones to beat

They are the best team in the world, the most attacking team in the world, they play the best football, have the best players, everyone wants to play like them and no one can stop them. (Or can they?) Spain are simply the best!

Above: There are few teams which can boast world superstars at every position; this Spanish squad can!

Since winning UEFA Euro 2008, Spain have gone on to dominate world football. They pass teams off the pitch with ease and are fast becoming one of the greatest teams of all time. They are so good they have their own unique style of football – "tiki-taka" – which not many teams have been able to stop.

Despite this new golden era, they haven't always been the masters of international football. They used to be one of the better teams in the world, but not quite the best, and would often find that anything past the group stages was a step too far.

However, they boast a fantastic record when it matters most; in four finals, they have only lost one, in 1984 when they lost to a France team captained by now-UEFA president Michel Platini. And they have qualified in style for the past two European Championships.

They qualified for Euro 2008 at the top of their group with 28 points out of a possible 36 and won all eight games of the 2012 qualifying campaign, scoring 26 goals and conceding a measly six. They booked their place at the Finals with a 6–0 victory over Liechtenstein. They won their group by a massive 11 points – scary!

At the 2008 Championships, not only did they win the tournament but they were the top-scoring team with 12 goals, David Villa finished top scorer with four goals, Xavi won player of the tournament and nine of the players were selected in the team of the tournament.

They have some of the best players in the world – the likes of Xavi, Andres Iniesta, David Silva and David Villa, to name just a few – and they should be the team everyone wants to copy when playing in the park!

No one will want to face Spain in the tournament because not only do they score lots of goals, but they are impossible to get the ball from. Teams who play Spain spend most of their time chasing shadows – and if they do manage to get the ball, they are instantly closed down as the whole team tries to win back the ball. This is Spain's era and their fans back home are loving every minute of it.

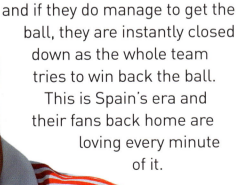

One to watch

Iker Casillas

The Spanish captain made his debut for the national side at the tender age of 19 and has been their number one for all of the 12 years since. A true winner, he has already won FIFA's World Cup and World Youth Championship, plus the UEFA European Championship and UEFA under-15 and under-16 titles. He is such a good keeper that he and Pepe Reina hold the national record for the longest time spent without conceding a goal, a massive 710 minutes! He always wears a short-sleeve goalkeeping shirt, whatever the weather, and he is a fantastic shot-stopper, often keeping Spain in games.

Meet the coach

Vicente del Bosque

The coach who may have the easiest job in world football, this 60-year-old is managing the best players and getting them to play the best football. Having guided Real Madrid to the UEFA Champions League in 2000 and 2002 and Spanish titles in 2001 and 2003, del Bosque replaced Luis Aragones after Spain won the UEFA Euro 2008 and immediately guided them to 2010 World Cup glory!

Italy
The proud Azurri

The most defensive side in world football, Italy have not won a European Championship since 1968. But don't let that record take away from the fact that they are one of the best teams in the world – and not many teams beat the Azzurri.

Above: Italy are always a hard team to score against, but many of their players can find the opposition's net.

Four-time World Champions and one-time European Champions, Italy are known as one of the most defensive sides in international football. If tournaments were won on who defended the best, then Italy would never lose!

When they won the World Cup back in 2006 they only conceded two goals, one being an open goal and the other a penalty.

During qualifying for Euro 2012, they also conceded two goals, this time in 10 games.

But they can also attack to great effect, as the Faroe Islands found out when Italy beat them 5–0. This makes Italy one of the hardest teams to face – they won't concede goals and they can score as many as they want.

The Azzurri tend to do better when looking for "firsts". They won the European Championship the first time they entered, back in 1964, and won the World Cup the first two times they played in the tournament in 1934 and 1938.

Although they don't have the same quality of defenders as they did in the past, they have an amazing goalkeeper in Gianluigi Buffon, the most expensive keeper ever when he went from Parma to Juventus for £30m and still one of the best shot-stoppers in the world.

Italy may not be as pretty to watch as Spain or Holland, but if you get them on FIFA 12 or the Euro 2012 game, you won't concede any goals!

Their midfield is full of players who like to make defence-splitting passes – Andrea Pirlo and Riccardo Montolivo like to dictate the play and Daniele De Rossi is like a wall; not much gets past him.

Then there's the unpredictable Mario Balotelli up front. When he's not playing with his iPad on the bench he's scoring amazing goals with his even more amazing haircuts. Put Giuseppe Rossi alongside him and you have a very good front two.

Manager Cesare Prandelli is attempting to build his own team, mixing youth with experience, and it is working. His side has beaten European and World Champions Spain in a friendly and he knows Italy can beat the top teams in the world.

Although they are not heavy favourites, they will definitely be one of the teams you would want to avoid meeting in the latter stages or going a goal down to, as you won't get many chances to equalize.

One to watch

Gianluigi Buffon

Seen as one of the greatest goalkeepers of all time, Gianluigi Buffon made his debut for Italy in 1997 as a substitute. It wasn't until Euro 2000 that he become the first choice but an injury before the tournament meant he was replaced by Francesco Toldo. He captained the national side to victory at World Cup 2006 where he only conceded two goals and kept five clean sheets. This will be his fourth appearance at the European Championships and he will be eager to lead his country to the final for the first time since 2000.

Meet the coach

Cesare Prandelli

Cesare Prandelli has overseen a changing of the guard in the Azzurri. The 54-year-old has brought in younger players and has Italy playing more attacking, free-flowing football. The longest-serving manager in Fiorentina history, Marcello Lippi's replacement has shown in his time with the Azzurri that promising signs are ahead and that may include UEFA Euro 2012!

Croatia
Red-and-White Delight

England's qualification conquerors in 2008 have gone further in the World Cup than the European Championship, despite two quarter-finals appearances, including in 2008. Three of their likely stars – Luka Modric, Vedran Corluka and Niko Kranjcar – were at Tottenham Hotspur in 2011.

Croatia are one of the most improved teams in Europe over the past 20 years – but that is hardly surprising seeing that they gained FIFA and UEFA recognition as recently as 1993! The nation had been part of the old Yugoslavia until it disintegrated in 1991, and Croatia claimed its independence in 1991.

Euro 96 was independent Croatia's first tournament, and they reached the last eight. But their best performance came at the 1998 World Cup, where they came third, after losing to eventual winners France in the semi-finals. The team was blessed with big, powerful defenders such as Slaven Bilic – now the national team coach – while, going forward, clever playmakers, including Zvonimir Boban (who spent 11 years at AC Milan) created chances for deadly strikers, such as Davor Suker.

The current squad may not be quite at that level yet, but there is plenty of talent and some

Above: Croatia have the flair and talent to upset the cream of European football in Poland and Ukraine in 2012.

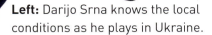

Left: Darijo Srna knows the local conditions as he plays in Ukraine.

awesome youngsters coming through the system. Experienced defenders Vedran Corluka and Josip Simunic are the leaders, but they will be battling against some exciting young talent for places at Euro 2012. Ivan Strinic, 24, plays in Ukraine for Dnipro, while centre-back Dejan Loveren, 22, and 20-year-old right-back Sime Vrsaljko have been linked with moves to Liverpool and Arsenal respectively.

Luka Modric is one of the best central midfielders in Europe today, while his Spurs team-mate Niko Kranjcar seems to score lots of goals when wearing the national shirt.

Mario Mandzukic could be Croatia's surprise package. The Wolfsburg striker scored two goals in the qualifiers, and hopes to add more in the finals. If he struggles, the experienced Ivica Olic and Eduardo should be able to supply some goals.

In the qualifying competition, Croatia were unbeaten at home, but were Group F runners-up behind Greece. The play-off against Turkey was decided in the first leg as Croatia rolled to a 3–0 win in Istanbul, and they coasted into the finals with a goalless draw in the return.

While they have lots of talented individuals, the fact that Croatia are a team going through a lot of changes means they will do well to get past the quarter-finals in Euro 2012.

One to watch

Darijo Srna

Darijo Srna is one of the best players to never play for one of Europe's biggest clubs. The Shakhtar Donetsk star is an incredibly versatile footballer, who is equally comfortable playing at right-back or right-midfield. While he is not a natural leader, in the style of John Terry or Carles Puyol, he leads by example. He is also one of the fittest players in the Croatia squad, and doesn't stop running for the whole 90 minutes. Srna has been strongly linked with English clubs Tottenham Hotspur and Chelsea, having been with Shakhtar since moving from Hajduk Split in 2003.

Meet the coach

Slaven Bilic

Slaven Bilic will go down as one the greatest defenders in Croatian history, remembered for blending power with style. After starting his career with hometown team Hajduk Split, he spent three years at Karlsruhe in Germany before enjoying success in the Premier League with West Ham and Everton. He finished his playing career back at Hajduk Split. He was appointed Croatia manager in 2006, and achieved success by qualifying for Euro 2008 at England's expense. This feat made him recognized as one of the world's best young managers. He also sings with rock band Rawbau and has a law degree!

Republic of Ireland

The boys in green

Ireland have only ever qualified for one European Championship finals – back in 1988. That's why their fans are so excited to reach Euro 2012, and they will cheer on their heroes with typical passion. It will surely spur on the team, and make it a tournament to remember for the boys in green!

Above: The Republic of Ireland may not be among the favourites, but they have a habit of causing upsets.

The European Championship qualifying competition has not been a happy hunting-ground for the Irish, who have reached only one finals, but often have gone very close.

Ireland went unbeaten in the Euro 92 qualifiers, but only one team went through and England finished one point above them. For Euro 96, they came unstuck against the Netherlands in a play-off, this after finishing runners-up in their group behind Portugal.

At Euro 88 Ireland finished third in their group after winning, drawing and losing against England, the Soviet Union and Holland respectively. The 1–0 win over England is one of Ireland's proudest sporting moments, with Ray Houghton's header dividing the sides.

Back to the present. This time Ireland finished two points behind Russia in qualification to secure their play-off position and were drawn against Estonia. Ireland romped to a 4–0 win in the away leg, with Robbie Keane scoring twice before they played out a 1–1 at home to win 5–1 on aggregate.

They scored 20 goals in qualifying, equalling their record for most goals in a Euro campaign, so if they can keep on firing at the same rate, summer 2012 could be fun!

If you are looking for a lucky omen – and there is always the luck of the Irish to consider – just remember that only two nations have ever gone 24 years between European Championship finals appearances, and both France and Greece celebrated by winning the whole tournament! And, of course, 2012 is 24 years after 1988.

The Republic of Ireland's team contains many Premier League stars, including goalkeeper Shay Given, key defenders Richard Dunne and John O'Shea, while performers such as Damien Duff, Seamus Coleman and Stephen Hunt provide the midfield with skill, flair and determination.

Jonathan Walters, Kevin Doyle and Leon Best are a trio of well-known Premier League strikers whom coach Giovanni Trapattoni can call upon in times of need, along with captain Keane. Fellow striker Aiden McGeady was playing further afield, for Spartak Moscow, but his experiences in the Champions League should help him as Ireland once more get to play on a major international stage.

Left: Giovanni Trapattoni's legendary reputation has grown with Ireland.

One to watch

Robbie Keane

It seems Robbie Keane has played for nearly as many clubs as he has scored goals, and with a scoring record as good as his, that's saying something! By the time Ireland had qualified he was the country's record goalscorer, with 53 goals in 113 games. Former manager Steve Staunton appointed Keane captain in 2006, and Giovanni Trapattoni kept him on in 2008. His time in England saw him play for Wolves, Coventry, Leeds, Spurs, Liverpool and West Ham, while other teams he has represented include Inter Milan and Celtic. He was playing for Los Angeles Galaxy at the time of qualification.

Meet the coach

Giovanni Trapattoni

Trapattoni won league titles in his native Italy – with Juventus and Inter Milan – Germany, Portugal and Austria, but was less successful as Italy's national coach at the 2002 World Cup and Euro 2004. He became Ireland manager in 2008 and might have steered them to the 2010 World Cup but for a controversial play-off defeat to France. He will be only the third man to coach two different teams at the European Championships, joining Russia's Dick Advocaat and Guus Hiddink.

Group C: Euro Stars

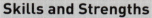

Country: Spain
Club: Barcelona
Position: Midfield
Born: 25 January 1980
Appearances: 107
Goals: 10

Xavi

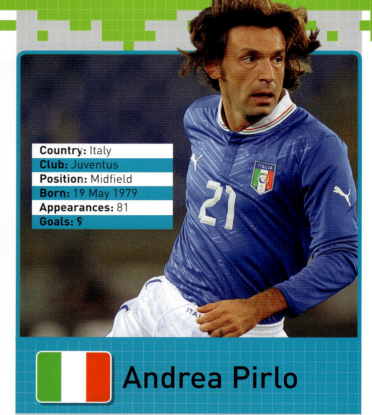

Country: Italy
Club: Juventus
Position: Midfield
Born: 19 May 1979
Appearances: 81
Goals: 9

Andrea Pirlo

Skills and Strengths

The heartbeat of the side, Xavi Hernandez (better known as Xavi) is vital to Spain. He gets them ticking and very rarely gives the ball away. He made the most passes at the 2010 World Cup and had a pass completion of 81 per cent.

Goals and Glory

It's easier to list what Xavi hasn't won than what he has. Part of the 2008 European Championship-winning team and a 2010 World Cup winner, he won "only" a silver medal at the Sydney 2000 Olympic Games. For his club, Barcelona, Xavi has won six La Liga titles, five Spanish super cups, three Champions Leagues, two UEFA super cups, and the Spanish cup and FIFA Club World Cup once each.

Claim to Fame

Xavi was named the La Liga breakthrough player of the season in 1999 and La Liga Spanish player of the season in 2005. He was in the FIFA and UEFA team of the year for three consecutive years (2008–10) and was also named the man of the match in the 2009 Champions League final. In the 2008 European Championships, he was in the team of the tournament and received the player of the tournament award.

Skills and Strengths

Many would say Andrea Pirlo, born in 1979, doesn't have many playing years left in him. However, Italians are known for playing into their late 30s and Pirlo's style of play suits that perfectly. Although he is not gifted with electrifying pace, it doesn't hinder his game as he lets the ball do all the running for him. He can pick out a player anywhere on the pitch and starts most of Italy's attacks. It is no wonder his team-mates have nicknamed him "l'architetto" (the architect).

Goals and Glory

Pirlo is a winner everywhere he goes. At AC Milan he won the Italian league twice (in 2004 and 2011), the Champions League and UEFA super cup also twice (in 2003 and 2007), the FIFA World Club Cup (2007), Italian cup (2003) and super cup (2004). On the international stage, he has helped Italy to win the 2000 European under-21 Championship, the World Cup in 2006 and he won a bronze medal at the 2004 Olympic Games.

Claim to Fame

Pirlo was the European under-21 Golden player and top scorer in 2004. He also made the 2006 World Cup team of the tournament as well as picking up the man of the match in the final.

Country:	Croatia
Club:	Tottenham Hotspur
Position:	Midfield
Born:	9 September 1985
Appearances:	52
Goals:	8

Luka Modric

Skills and Strengths
Creative midfielder Luka Modric is one of the world's best all-round players. He passes well, works hard and has also improved his tackling since moving to the Premier League. Even though he's quite small, he is still strong enough to mix it with much bigger players.

Goals and Glory
As an individual, Modric has won many awards. Last season he was named Tottenham's player of the season and at Euro 2008 he was named in the team of the tournament. He previously won the Croatian league's player of the year award. During his time with Dinamo Zagreb he won the Croatian league three times and the national cup twice. In his first season with Tottenham, he reached the final of the League Cup. Success on the international stage has, so far, eluded Modric, but he is only 26 and Croatia are a rising power; so, who knows?

Claim to Fame
Modric's excellent performances made him a wanted man in the Premier League, particularly at Chelsea, who made a number of bids for him. On the last day of the 2011 summer transfer window, Chelsea bid £40m for him but Tottenham rejected this.

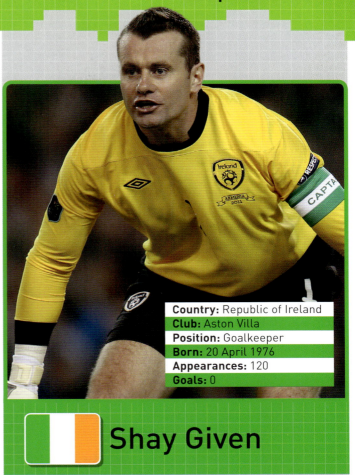

Country:	Republic of Ireland
Club:	Aston Villa
Position:	Goalkeeper
Born:	20 April 1976
Appearances:	120
Goals:	0

Shay Given

Skills and Strengths
Shay Given is one of the most admired goalkeepers in the world, with agility, reflexes and shot-stopping ability beyond the level of most ordinary custodians. Ireland captain Robbie Keane has called Given "the best goalkeeper in the Premier League" – and many of his former managers would agree. The 36-year-old will relish the chance to represent Ireland on the world stage and prove his ability yet again. The boys in green know they can call on him to perform as the last line of defence.

Goals and Glory
The outstanding performances produced by Given have not brought him the trophies and medals they deserved, and the 2011 FA Cup winner's medal is his only prestigious award – and even that came only as a substitute, for Manchester City. Given won the First Division title with Sunderland (in 1996) and the InterToto Cup with Newcastle (in 2006).

Claim to Fame
Individual awards for Given include the Irish senior international player of the year (in 2005 and 2006), Newcastle player of the year (2006), and the Premier League team of the season (2002 and 2006).

Ukraine
Determined to shine

Ukraine are co-hosts of UEFA Euro 2012 along with Poland and this will be their first-ever European Championship finals. So the pressure is really on for Oleg Blokhin's side to put on a good show in front of their home fans.

Ukraine only started life as an independent state in 1992 following the break-up of the old Soviet Union so there will be huge national pride involved when they kick off a major Finals in their own country.

Fans in Kiev and across the country will be hoping they can cheer their team to success because results up to now, to say the least, have been rather disappointing.

Ukraine failed to qualify for either UEFA Euro 2008 or the World Cup in South Africa in 2010 and recent friendly results have been worrying – including defeats against the Czech Republic, Uruguay, Sweden, France, Italy and Brazil.

You can see from that list of opponents, however, that Ukraine have been preparing for the Finals (as hosts they don't need to qualify) by playing against some of the toughest teams in the world; and maybe that experience will stand them in good stead when the action gets underway for real.

Above: Ukraine want home advantage to make their first European Championship finals memorable.

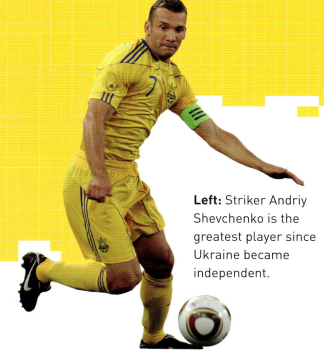

Left: Striker Andriy Shevchenko is the greatest player since Ukraine became independent.

The atmosphere in stadiums during UEFA Euro 2012 should certainly give them a boost – and Champions League clubs across Europe already know how difficult it is to win in Kiev or Donetsk.

They can also look back on happy memories of the 2006 World Cup in Germany when Ukraine, then also under the guidance of current coach Blokhin who is now in his second spell as head coach, reached the last eight, only losing in the end to eventual champions Italy.

In those days, however, star striker Andriy Shevchenko (who moved to Chelsea for £30m after the 2006 World Cup Finals) was in his pomp. These days he is 34 and will certainly need some help up front if Ukraine are to make an impact.

Maybe Bayern Munich midfielder Anatoliy Tymoshchuk will prove influential, or perhaps Dynamo Moscow's experienced striker Andriy Voronin can chip in. Either way, Ukraine will need a swift improvement in fortunes if they are to make a challenge on home soil.

One to watch

Andriy Shevchenko

At the age of 34, this could be legendary striker Shevchenko's last major tournament – and he will want to make the most of it. Now playing back in his home country for Dinamo Kiev (where his career took off), the former AC Milan and Chelsea man is still a big hero. Things did not go well for him at Stamford Bridge but he won the UEFA Champions League with Milan in 2003, scored an incredible 67 Champions League goals and was European player of the year in 2004. It's not surprising he is such a hero in his home country. He has scored 45 goals in 102 games in international football so far and is currently the captain!

Meet the coach

Oleg Blokhin

The 58-year-old was a superstar striker for Dinamo Kiev and the Soviet Union, and he has turned out to be a great coach too! Blokhin was a hugely famous name in the 1970s – even being named European player of the year in 1975 – and he ended his career as his league's record goal-scorer with 211 goals. This is his second spell as coach of Ukraine, having been in charge 2003–07, reaching the quarter-finals of the 2006 World Cup. Now his big dream is to lead them to glory on home soil at UEFA Euro 2012.

England
The new generation

England did not qualify for Euro 2008 and have never won the European Championship. However, as long as they can avoid Portugal or a penalty shoot-out and keep Wayne Rooney on the pitch long enough, the Three Lions hope to go far this time!

Above: England want to turn their undefeated qualifying campaign into a winning run in Poland and Ukraine.

Winning a major tournament takes skill and luck, something England are yet to experience in great measure! But whether it is ability or a lack of fortune, the fact remains that they have failed to pass the group stages on four attempts. And they will have to get through most of the group stages this time without key striker Wayne Rooney, suspended for the first two games following his sending-off in England's final qualification game in Montenegro.

England have twice advanced from the group stages, and then been knocked out on penalties. In 1996 it was in the semi-final against Germany and, in the 2004 quarter-finals, Portugal's goalkeeper Ricardo saved a penalty and then scored with the next kick to send England home!

European Championships and Portugal do not go together well for England; in 2000 they lost 3–2 after being 2–0 up and in 2004 Rooney was injured in the quarter-finals and was England's and the competition's top scorer at the time. England later went on to lose that game on penalties.

But since 2004 there has been a growing sense that England have improved and once again are one of the major forces in international football. After a disappointing 2010 World Cup, Fabio Capello's successor as coach will have a new-look side. A younger, more vibrant England team is expected in Poland–Ukraine with youngsters such as Jack Wilshere, Phil Jones, Chris Smalling and Joe Hart all exciting during their qualifying campaign.

Expect to see the usual England faces as well, though, and that means Rooney, John Terry, Ashley Cole, Rio Ferdinand and Steven Gerrard will all be vital to England's plans, and their experience will be needed to help the younger players get used to playing in a major tournament.

England scored 17 goals in their eight qualifying group games, including beating Bulgaria 4–0 at home and 3–0 away. This team knows how to score goals so they will be a team to avoid in the draw for the group stages – with or without Rooney!

Left: Theo Walcott (7), Jermain Defoe and Steven Gerrard (4) can all contribute goals for England in 2012.

One to watch

Steven Gerrard

Steven Gerrard has been one of England's best performers since his debut in 2000. The Liverpool player captained his country at the 2010 World Cup and is considered one of the most inspirational figures in the squad. Gerrard, who will be just 32 when Euro 2012 starts, has been one of the best midfielders in European football for the last 10 years and has spent his entire career at Liverpool, winning the Champions League, UEFA Cup and FA Cup. He is a tough tackler who drives his team-mates on from midfield and chips in with assists and goals.

Meet the coach

Stuart Pearce

Stuart Pearce is England through and through. He was a fan-favourite in his England playing days and had the nickname "Psycho"! Fabio Capello was due to lead England at Euro 2012, but he resigned in February. Pearce took on the role on a temporary basis before the FA appointed the next permanent manager. He was a prime candidate for the role after his sterling work as coach of the England under-21 team and Capello's assistant.

Sweden
Leading Scandinavians

Runners-up in the 1958 World Cup, semi-finalists in the 1992 European Championships and 1994 World Cup, the only major competition Sweden have won to date is the 1948 Olympics. Although outsiders for the tournament, they have the players to cause a real upset in 2012.

Above: Sweden have been international tournament threats before and they might be Euro 2012 dark horses.

One thing is for sure, past Swedish teams knew what it took to go all the way in international tournaments and it is something that this team will be looking to do in Poland–Ukraine.

It is difficult to determine what their career highlight is – playing Brazil in the World Cup final in Sweden in 1958, or winning gold at the 1948 Olympics in England, with an English manager in George Raynor?

In 1992, Sweden reached the semi-finals of the European Championships. Tournament hosts, they qualified top of a group consisting of Denmark, France and England. Wonder if that would be the same now?

They lost 3–2 to Germany in the semi-finals, but the disappointment of the result did not last too long, as they picked themselves up two years later and managed to reach the semi-finals of the World Cup in the USA.

This was another great tournament as they finished second of a group with Brazil, Russia and Cameroon. How many teams can say that they have done that before?

Even though they lost to Brazil in the semis, it is nothing to be ashamed of. And they only lost 1–; some teams have done a lot worse when facing the Yellow of Brazil.

In Zlatan Ibrahimovic, they have one of the most feared strikers on the planet. Sweden's captain was his team's top scorer with five goals and it might have been more had he not been suspended for the final group game.

And with midfielder Kim Kallstrom – whose seven assists were joint best in the qualifying competition – providing him with chances, Sweden will be a dangerous outfit in Poland and Ukraine.

They reached the finals in style by beating the Netherlands 3–2 in their final match to end the group winners' perfect record. Sweden's 31 goals was third-best in qualifying – behind the Dutch and Germany – and 24 points gave them automatic qualification as the best runners-up in the nine groups.

Left: Erik Hamren was a winner at club level and is looking to repeat that success on the international stage.

One to watch

Zlatan Ibrahimovic

Zlatan Ibrahimovic won eight consecutive league titles with five different clubs: Ajax [2004], Juventus [2005 and 2006], Inter Milan [from 2007 to 2009], Barcelona [2010] and AC Milan [2011]. His lanky physique is deceptive. He is tall and wins lots of headers, but he's more dangerous with the ball at his feet. He likes to take on players with his dribbling skills before calmly shooting past the goalkeeper. It is no wonder that Ibrahimovic was Serie A's top scorer in 2009 and, as Sweden's main threat, he will need to be at his very best to help his country do well at Euro 2012.

Meet the coach

Erik Hamren

Few managers can handle the pressure of managing two teams at once, but Erik Hamren can, and he did so in two countries. When he became Sweden's coach in November 2009, he was still in charge of Norway's Rosenborg, winning the league in both 2009 and 2010. Hamren has years of experience as a coach, winning the Swedish cup with Orgryte and the Danish league with Aalborg, so nothing the European Championships have to offer will surprise him. And he will be hoping teams don't take Sweden too seriously, so he can spring a few surprises on them!

France
Allez les Bleus

Two-time European champions, France are one of the best teams in the competition and trail only three-time champions Germany. The first team to host and win the tournament, in 1984, Les Bleus last won it in 2000. All eyes will be on them as they are hosting Euro 2016.

France won their first European championship in 1984 – and what a tournament it was! The host nation won all of their group games and, after a tight semi-final against Portugal, beat Spain 2–0 in the final to become the first nation to win the tournament on home soil.

In that squad was the current president of UEFA, Michel Platini. He was the tournament's top scorer with nine goals, including the opening goal in the final.

France's next triumphant team, 14 years later, did not have it so easy. They qualified second in their group behind the Netherlands and their semi-final against Portugal went to extra time. They faced Italy in the final and, after going a goal behind, striker Sylvain Wiltord scored in the 94th minute to send the game to extra time.

At the time, matches were settled by the golden goal rule, with the first team to score

Above: France may have been among the fourth seeds in the Euro 2012 draw, but their recent form is impressive.

winning – and it was French striker David Trezeguet who struck in the 103rd minute.

Current Les Bleus coach Laurent Blanc started that match, so has first-hand experience at winning the tournament, which could prove to be important in the later stages.

Many fans will remember France for their world-class players such as Zinedine Zidane and Thierry Henry. Although neither now plays for their national team, the French squad is currently blessed with a large number of talented players.

Defender Mamadou Sakho is one of the hottest prospects in Europe at the moment and midfielder Yoann Gourcuff was dubbed the "next Zidane" – not a bad player to be likened to. Also in the midfield is Samir Nasri, another player who has been labelled the next Zidane. To have two players similar to a former three-time FIFA world player of the year is quite impressive!

With the players Blanc has at his disposal, he has the talent to match the 1984 and 2000 European Champions. His team qualified for Euro 2012 on the final day of the qualifying group stage with a 1–1 draw against Bosnia and Herzegovina. They picked up six wins in their 10 matches and conceded only four goals.

Right: Coach Lauren Blanc has turned around the French team's fortunes in just two years.

One to watch

Hugo Lloris

Hugo Lloris, 24, is considered one of the world's best goalkeepers. After a superb 2010 World Cup, he was appointed captain and has continued to improve. A two-time French goalkeeper of the year, he is also a European Under-19 Football Championship winner. That experience, coupled with years of Champions League exploits for Lyon, could be vital in Poland and Ukraine. His lightning reflexes, amazing ability at saving one-on-ones, and excellent decision-making will make him a very difficult goalkeeper to beat. Young for an international goalkeeper, Lloris has represented France at every age group.

Meet the coach

Laurent Blanc

One of the most stylish international coaches, Laurent Blanc can be seen in designer glasses and suit with a white stick in his mouth – often a lollipop! Nicknamed Le President due to his strong leadership skills, Blanc has revolutionized French football with a more attacking and fluid style of play. And being a World Cup and European Championship winner as a player (though he was suspended for the 1998 World Cup final), Blanc has the credentials to lead France to glory.

Group D: Euro Stars

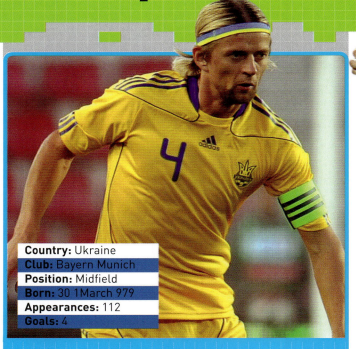

Country: Ukraine
Club: Bayern Munich
Position: Midfield
Born: 30 1March 979
Appearances: 112
Goals: 4

Anatoliy Tymoshchuk

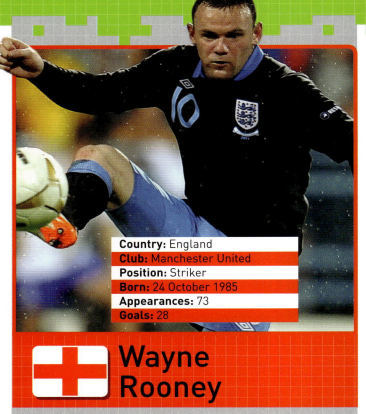

Country: England
Club: Manchester United
Position: Striker
Born: 24 October 1985
Appearances: 73
Goals: 28

Wayne Rooney

Skills and Strengths

Anatoliy Tymoshchuk is a solid defensive midfielder for both club and country. He has great ball-holding skills, strength and the ability to pick out a long ball off both feet, and can also go forward to provide his team with assists. This would be useful if he is used as playmaker behind captain and striker Andriy Shevchenko and could be Ukraine's perfect formula for goals.

Goals and Glory

Tymoshchuk has a full trophy cabinet from his time with Shakhtar Donetsk, Zenit St Petersburg and Bayern Munich, winning the league with each team. At Shakhtar, he won three league (in 2002, 2005 and 2006) and cup (in 2001, 2002 and 2004) winner's medals and won Ukraine's super cup (in 2005). With Zenit, he won Russia's premier league in 2007 and Russia's super cup, the UEFA Cup and UEFA Super Cup all in 2008. The 2010 season with Bayern was his best yet, as he enjoyed a clean sweep of domestic trophies, the German league, cup and super cup, and collected a Champions League runners-up medal.

Claim to Fame

The dynamic midfielder has been Ukraine's footballer of the year three times (in 2002, 2006 and 2007).

Skills and Strengths

Able to play as a lone striker or as a playmaker behind a striker, Wayne Rooney offers England so much. He can set up goals as well as score them and it doesn't matter whether it's a long-range strike or a simple tap in. He scored four goals in England's Euro 2004 campaign before being injured in the quarter-finals and England will be hoping he can repeat that form when his two-match suspension is completed in the group stage.

Goals and Glory

At club level with Manchester United, Rooney has won almost everything: four league titles, two League Cups, the UEFA Champions League and FIFA World Club Cup. It's no surprise, then, that when he signed a new contract with United in 2010, it made him the highest-paid player at the club.

Claim to Fame

Rooney was named in the Euro 2004 team of the tournament and won the PFA players' player of the year, PFA young player of the year twice and PFA fans' player of the year twice. At the start of the 2011–12 season, he scored back-to-back hat-tricks against Arsenal and Bolton, only the fourth player in Premier League history to do so.

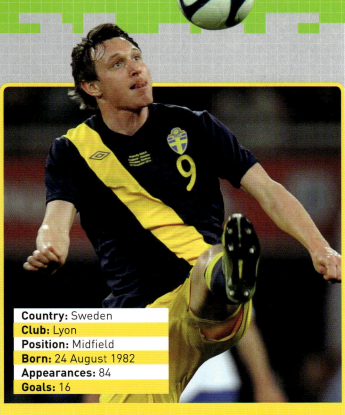

Country: Sweden
Club: Lyon
Position: Midfield
Born: 24 August 1982
Appearances: 84
Goals: 16

Kim Kallstrom

Skills and Strengths

Known worldwide as a playmaker to watch out for, Kim Kallstrom can be the vital ingredient to supply goal after goal to the likes of Zlatan Ibrahimovic. At 29, the midfielder is at the peak of his career and looks certain to be a vital presence at the centre of the Swedish squad.

Goals and Glory

Kallstrom finished the Euro 2012 qualifying competition as joint-top of the assists table with seven, sharing that accolade with Germany's Mesut Ozil. At club level, he helped Lyon to two French league titles (in 2007 and 2008), the French cup in 2008 and the French super cup in 2006 and 2007. In Sweden, Kallstrom collected winner's medals in the league twice (in 2002 and 2003) and the cup (also in 2002), all with Djurgarden.

Claim to Fame

In the final qualifying group match for Euro 2012, Kallstrom opened the scoring for Sweden as their 3–2 victory over the Netherlands automatically sent his country to the finals as best runners-up. At club level, he scored 14 goals in 26 matches for Djurgarden when they won the Swedish league title in 2003.

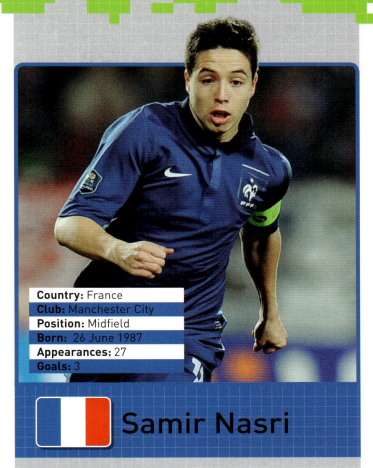

Country: France
Club: Manchester City
Position: Midfield
Born: 26 June 1987
Appearances: 27
Goals: 3

Samir Nasri

Skills and Strengths

Samir Nasri's vision, technical skill and ability to read and understand the game have made him one of the best playmakers in world football. Labelled as the next Zinedine Zidane, thanks not only to his Algerian heritage but also his elegance on the ball, the 24-year-old (he turns 25 during the finals) has the ability and flair to unpick any defence – and this could be vital for France in tight games.

Goals and Glory

Part of France's under-17 squad that won the European Championship in 2004, Nasri knows what it is like to win an international tournament. And at club level he helped Marseille to win the UEFA Intertoto Cup (2005), so he has what it takes to go all the way in knockout competitions. His equalizing goal against Bosnia in the last Euro 2012 qualifying match sent France through to the finals as group winners.

Claim to Fame

Nasri won the French player of the year award in 2010, having been the French top division's player of the year in 2007, and in their 2007 Ligue 1 team of the season too. In 2011, before moving from Arsenal to Manchester City, he was in the PFA Premier League team of the season.

Euro 2012 Picture Quiz

They say every picture tells a story. Can you work out what's what in the following footy foursomes?

Captain Fantastic
Who are the following leaders of men, and what countries do they play for?

A

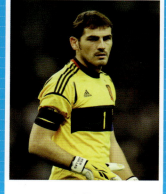

B

C

D

Demons of the dug-out
Who are the Svengalis going through hell on the touchline, and what countries will they be attempting to guide to glory at Euro 2012?

A

B

C

D

So glad we've made it!

Which teams are obviously over the moon to have qualified for the finals of Euro 2012, and who did they knock out in the process?

A

B

C

D

Trip down memory lane

Can you name the year of the European Championships depicted below and the exultant winners of the Henri Delaunay trophy in each case?

A

B

C

D

Euro 2012 Trivia Quiz

So you think you're pretty clued up about the UEFA European Championships. Test your knowledge with this monster UEFA EURO quiz. You'll find the answers on the next page. But no sneaky peeking! I thought you knew your Waddles from your Hoddles.

1 Who is Spain's first-choice goalkeeper?

A   Cesc Fabregas ☐
B   Iker Casillas ☐
C   Heurelho Gomes ☐
D   Carles Puyol ☐

2 What is the nickname of the Polish football team?

A   White Lions ☐
B   Red Lions ☐
C   Red Eagles ☐
D   White Eagles ☐

3 Which of these Euro 2012 finalists has a capital city situated on the River Dnieper?

A   Ukraine ☐
B   Germany ☐
C   Poland ☐
D   Russia ☐

4 Who is the Republic of Ireland's leading goalscorer?

A   Roy Keane ☐
B   Robbie Keane ☐
C   Niall Quinn ☐
D   David Healy ☐

5 Who is the all-time top Polish goalscorer?

A   Grzegorz Lato ☐
B   Kazimierz Denya ☐
C   Wlodzimierz Lubanski ☐
D   Jan Tomaszewski ☐

6 Who are the current UEFA European champions?

A   Germany ☐
B   Spain ☐
C   France ☐
D   Greece ☐

7 Which of the 16 finalists was highest in the FIFA world rankings at the time of the Euro 2012 draw?

A   Germany ☐
B   Italy ☐
C   Holland ☐
D   Spain ☐

8 Which of the 16 finalists was lowest in the FIFA world rankings at the time of the Euro 2012 draw?

A   Republic of Ireland ☐
B   Ukraine ☐
C   Poland ☐
D   Denmark ☐

9 Who is the Italian coach?

A   Giovanni Trapattoni ☐
B   Fabio Capello ☐
C   Flavia Cacace ☐
D   Cesare Prandelli ☐

10 What are the names of the pair of Euro 2012 mascots?

A   Lech and Yuri ☐
B   Borscht and Schnitzel ☐
C   Svetlana and Saskia ☐
D   Slavek and Slavko ☐

11 What are the two colours of the Ukrainian national flag?

A   Yellow and blue ☐
B   Red and white ☐
C   Blue and white ☐
D   Yellow and white ☐

12 What is the capital city of Ukraine?

A   Krakow ☐
B   Odessa ☐
C   Kyiv ☐
D   Vladivostok ☐

13 Which football administrator founded the UEFA European Championship?

A Jules Rimet
B Pierre de Courbertin
C Franz Beckenbauer
D Henri Delaunay

14 Who is the President of UEFA?

A Sepp Blatter
B Michel Platini
C Grzegorz Lato
D Lennart Johansson

15 Who was sent off for England in their final Euro 2012 qualifying game?

A John Terry
B David Beckham
C Wayne Rooney
D Ashley Cole

16 Which of these teams wasn't knocked out in the Euro 2012 play-offs.

A Montenegro
B Estonia
C Serbia
D Turkey

17 Which two former winners of the European Championship meet on 9 June in Kharkiv?

A Denmark and Netherlands
B Germany and Spain
C France and Italy
D Greece and Czech Republic

18 Which Dutch Eurostar plays up front for Arsenal.

A Wesley Sneijder
B Robin van Persie
C Dirk Kuyt
D Niklas Bendtner

19 How many games will there be in total at Euro 2012?

A 64
B 32
C 31
D 24

20 When will the Final of Euro 2012 take place?

A 1 June
B 30 June
C 4 July
D 1 July

21 Which pair of countries listed below share a border with both Poland and Ukraine?

A Bulgaria and Hungary
B Belarus and Slovakia
C Czech Republic and Romania
D Moldova and Austria

22 Which one of these Euro 2012 stadiums is located in Poland?

A PGE Arena
B Olympic Stadium
C Metalist Stadium
D Donbass Arena

23 What is the capital city of Poland?

A Gdansk
B Smolensk
C Warsaw
D Minsk

24 Who was the top scorer in the Euro 2012 qualifiers with 12 goals?

A Miroslav Klose
B Robbie Keane
C Cristiano Ronaldo
D Klaas Jan Huntlaar

25 Who spoiled Holland's perfect record in the final qualifying match in Group E?

A Germany
B Sweden
C Turkey
D Greece

26 Who scored a hat-trick in the Euro 2012 qualifiers for Sweden against Finland?

A Kim Kallstgrom
B Emir Bajrami
C Zlatan Ibrahimovic
D Erik Hamren

27 In which Euro 2012 host city is St Sophia's Cathedral?

A Poznan
B Kyiv
C Krakow
D Lviv

28 Group B Euro 2012 will comprise which four teams?

A Holland • Germany • Croatia • Denmark
B Holland • Germany • Portugal • Denmark
C Germany • England • Portugal • Denmark
D Holland • Germany • Portugal • Republic of Ireland

29 Who were the last team to be chosen in the draw for the finals of Euro 2012?

A England
B Czech Republic
C Republic of Ireland
D Denmark

30 Which two teams will play in the opening match of Euro 2012?

A Poland and Greece
B Poland and Russia
C Ukraine and England
D Ukraine and France

Euro 2012 Crossword

Across

1 Rangers midfielder whose two goals in the qualifiers failed to get Scotland to Euro 2012 **(5)**

3 Nationality of players who finished behind the Danes and Portuguese in the Euro 2012 qualifiers **(9)**

6 Country that saw off Montenegro and Bulgaria to qualify for Euro 2012 **(7)**

8 French Ligue 1 team for whom Le Guen, Ginola and 16A once played **(5)**

10 Providing Euro 2012 with the likes of Evra, Nani and Jones **(6)**

11 Everton and Belgium midfielder who failed to power his side to Euro 2012 qualification **(8)**

12 Though born in Glasgow, this Spartak Moscow winger hopes to fire the Republic of Ireland to success in Poland and Ukraine **(5,7)**

16 Bayern Munich winger whom Zidane called the jewel of French football **(6,6)**

18 Serbian SuperLiga side from Belgrade **(8)**

19 Charlton Athletic's famous old ground, the ... **(6)**

22 Polish international keeper warming the bench at Real **(5)**

23 Rubin Kazan striker first named in the Russian squad in October 2011 **(7)**

24 Bayern Munich left-footer who scored v Azerbaijan in the Euro qualifiers **(9)**

25 Second only to Berbatov in the all-time Bulgarian national scoring charts **(5)**

Down

1 Official name of the European championship trophy, the Henri ... Cup **(8)**

2 23 goals in 49 games for 17D, Bobo retired from football in 2009 **(5)**

3 Ex-Liverpool full-back, right-hand man to Graham Taylor in 1994 **(4)**

4 UEFA European Championship winners in 1972, '80 and '96 **(7)**

5 Providing Euro 2012 with the likes of Mertesacker, Rosicky and Sagna **(7)**

7 Colour adorning the Republic of Ireland shirts **(5)**

9 551-game Fluminense defender, a Brazil World Cup winner back in 1962 **(6)**

13 Won two World Cups with 17D, San Siro was renamed after him in 1980 **(6)**

14 Zenit St Petersburg and Russia midfielder named in the Euro 2008 Team of the Tournament **(8)**

15 La Liga side from Naverre with whom Sammy Lee once had a spell **(7)**

16 Level of physical health key to Euro 2012 success **(7)**

17 European Championship winners in 1968 **(5)**

20 Statesman whose name once adorned Moscow's Luzhniki Stadium **(5)**

21 Republic of Ireland right-back, captain of Birmingham City **(4)**

Answers

Euro 2012 Picture Quiz

Captain Fantastic
A Andriy Shevchenko (Ukraine)
B Philipp Lahm (Germany)
C Iker Casillas (Spain)
D Marc van Bommel (Netherlands)

So glad we've made it!
A Croatia (Turkey)
B Czech Republic (Montenegro)
C Portugal (Bosnia and Herzegovina)
D Republic of Ireland (Estonia)

Demons of the dug-out
A Slaven Bilic (Croatia)
B Joachim Low (Germany)
C Vicente del Bosque (Spain)
D Oleg Blokhin (Ukraine)

Trip down memory lane
A 1992 (Denmark)
B 2008 (Spain)
C 1988 (Netherlands)
D 2004 (Greece)

Euro 2012 Trivia Quiz

1 Iker Casillas. 2 White Eagles. 3 Ukraine. 4 Robbie Keane. 5 Wlodzimierz Lubanski. 6 Spain. 7 Spain. 8 Poland. 9 Cesare Prandelli. 10 Slavek and Slavko. 11 Yellow and blue. 12 Kyiv. 13 Henri Delaunay. 14 Michel Platini. 15 Wayne Rooney. 16 Serbia. 17 Denmark and Netherlands. 18 Robin van Persie. 19 31. 20 1 July. 21 Belarus and Slovakia. 22 PGE Arena (Gdansk). 23 Warsaw. 24 Klaas Jan Huntelaar. 25 Sweden. 26 Zlatan Ibrahimovic. 27 Kyiv. 28 Holland • Germany • Portugal • Denmark. 29 England. 30 Poland and Russia.

Euro 2012 Crossword

Answers on page 2

Euro 2012 Fill-in Chart

Fill in the results from the matches as they are played and watch as the tournament unfolds. Will your team live up to the expectations piled on them, will they fail miserably, or will 1 July be a night of national glory?

Note: These kick-off times are CET. Kick-off times in Ukraine are 19:00 and 21:45; in Britain and Republic of Ireland, they are 17:00 and 19:45.

Group A

Group	Match	Date/time	Venue	Fixture	Score	
A	1	Fri 8 June / 18:00	Warsaw	Poland v Greece		
	2	Fri 8 June / 20:45	Wroclaw	Russia v Czech Republic		
	9	Tue 12 June / 18:00	Wroclaw	Greece v Czech Republic		
	10	Tue 12 June / 20:45	Warsaw	Poland v Russia		
	17	Sat 16 June / 20:45	Wroclaw	Czech Republic v Poland		
	18	Sat 16 June / 20:45	Warsaw	Greece v Russia		

FINAL TABLE

	Team	P	W	D	L	F	A	Pts	Top scorer
1		3							
2		3							
3		3							
4		3							

Group B

Group	Match	Date/time	Venue	Fixture	Score	
B	3	Sat 9 June / 18:00	Kharkiv	Netherlands v Denmark		
	4	Sat 9 June / 20:45	Lviv	Germany v Portugal		
	11	Wed 13 June / 18:00	Lviv	Denmark v Portugal		
	12	Wed 13 June / 20:45	Kharkiv	Netherlands v Germany		
	19	Sun 17 June / 20:45	Kharkiv	Portugal v Netherlands		
	20	Sun 17 June / 20:45	Lviv	Denmark v Germany		

FINAL TABLE

	Team	P	W	D	L	F	A	Pts	Top scorer
1		3							
2		3							
3		3							
4		3							